ASK PASTOR DARRYL

Answers to 121 Frequently Asked
Bible Questions

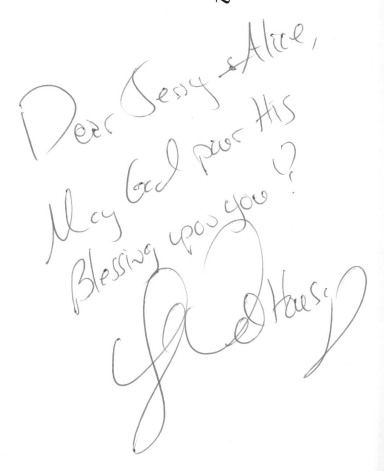

Dear Jessy–Alice,

May God pour His

Blessing upon you ?

ASK PASTOR DARRYL

Answers to 121 Frequently Asked Bible Questions

Darryl DelHousaye
and
Bobby Brewer

Edited by Randy Sampson

SBC PRESS • SCOTTSDALE, ARIZONA
2002

Cover design: Steve Brown
Book design and typesetting: Randy Sampson
Back cover photos: Richard Voit

Printed and bound in the United States of America
by Sheridan Books, Inc.

ISBN 0-9724328-0-9

SBC Press
7601 East Shea Boulevard
Scottsdale, Arizona 85260-5500

All profits from the sale of this book go to
Scottsdale Bible Church's "Enlarge Our Hearts
to Reach the Lost" campaign.

This book is dedicated to Scottsdale Bible Church and to all of you who asked the questions.

Contents

Acknowledgements

Holly DelHousaye, what a great idea.

The people of SBC who asked the questions.

Special thanks to the following for sharing in their particular areas of expertise:

Randy Sampson, Editor, and book design and typesetting; B.A. in Christian Education, *summa cum laude*, North Central University; A.B.S., Moody Bible Institute; A.A.S. in Computer Usage and Technology, Rio Salado Community College.

Steve Brown, cover design; Minister of Evangelism and Discipleship, Scottsdale Bible Church.

Dr. Jacque Chadwick, Chairman of the Board, Phoenix Seminary; Vice Dean, Phoenix Campus, College of Medicine, University of Arizona.

Dr. Paul Wegner, Professor of Old Testament, Phoenix Seminary (B.A., Moody Bible Institute; M.Div., Th.M., Trinity Evangelical Divinity School; Ph.D., University of London).

Cathy Wilson, Chosen People—Scottsdale.

Finally, thanks to our other volunteer proofreaders: Amy Ables, Kristen Brewer, Shirley Brewer, Jill Clark, Wendy Meredith, and Orville Weyrich.

It was Holly, my wife, who suggested that we have a place on our church's newly formed website (scottsdalebible.com) where people could send me their questions about the Bible by e-mail. Little did we know that it would receive such a favorable reaction. As a pastor, I am very encouraged that you have questions relating to how you can apply God's Word to your everyday life. The Bible itself is the final authority and arbitrator, and thus it is possible that we may be off in some cases of nonessential Christian doctrine. However, with the help of Bobby Brewer I have done my best at answering some of the most frequently asked questions about the Bible that we receive, and so my prayer is that this book will shed some light on a number of controversial, mysterious, and confusing issues that are often raised.

I also want to express my gratitude to you for purchasing this book, of which 100% of the proceeds will go toward our "Enlarge Our Hearts to Reach the Lost" campaign. It is also my prayer that, like the Bereans, you will continue to search and examine the Scriptures in your pursuit of becoming a student of God's Word.

Walk Worthy,

Darryl DelHousaye
Senior Pastor
Scottsdale Bible Church

ABBREVIATIONS

KJV King James Version

NASB New American Standard Bible

NIV New International Version

NKJV New King James Version

NT New Testament

OT Old Testament

SBC Scottsdale Bible Church

Abortion

Q: What is your position on abortion? What does the Bible have to say about it?

A: The Bible reveals that humans are unique because they are created and formed in God's image (Gen. 1:27). Thus our foremost appeal for an answer is at the legal bar of God's Word where scientific facts are coordinate expressions of truth and where definition and precedent are consistent with original decrees. One of the key issues in the debate about abortion is *When does life begin?* Based upon the Bible and scientific evidence it is clear that human life begins at conception. Consider the following:

The Hebrew word for "child" refers to postnatal life in Exodus 21:4. Yet it also translates "a woman with child" in Exodus 21:22, referring to prenatal existence.

John the Baptist is referred to as a child (*brephos*, Lk. 1:41,44) in his prenatal period. The same term is used with reference to the infants slaughtered by Pharaoh after their birth (Acts 7:19).

Thus there is evidence from both the Old and New Testaments that demonstrates that the Bible understands personhood to exist prior to birth. Likewise, to say that one does not become a person until birth is to say that God forms non-persons in the womb. While the Bible is not a manual on embryology, it does make explicit statements that personhood begins in the womb.

> For Thou didst form my inward parts; Thou didst weave me in my
> mother's womb. I will give thanks to Thee, for I am fearfully and
> wonderfully made; wonderful are Thy works, and my soul knows it
> very well. My frame was not hidden from Thee, when I was made in

secret, and skillfully wrought in the depths of the earth (Ps. 139:13-15).

Interestingly, God consecrated Jeremiah as a prophet while he was in the womb (Jer. 1:5). Jeremiah later declared that if he had died before birth his mother's womb would have become his grave (Jer. 20:17). Therefore, the death of Jeremiah in the womb would have been the death of God's prophet, not a non-person.

Christ was born in the manner of men (Gal. 4:4) and in the likeness of humanity (Heb. 2:17). Because Christ did not cease to be a person as a fetus, we can conclude that all who are conceived in the human womb are persons from conception. Therefore, we can assuredly conclude that the Bible is clear on this matter: Life begins with conception, and therefore abortion is contrary to God's moral expectations and is in fact the murdering of a human (Ex. 20:13; Mt. 5:21-22; 1 Jn. 3:15). This is also one of the reasons why we support the Crisis Pregnancy Centers of Greater Phoenix and the Christian Family Care Agency. In addition to providing an alternative to abortion (adoption), they also provide excellent counseling as well as post- abortion care.

Q: I am sure you have heard of the great debate over the issue of using otherwise discarded human embryos for research purposes. As a Christian medical researcher, I have been struggling with this issue. Is it okay considering that the embryos would otherwise be discarded? What do you the church or the Bible have to say about this subject?

A: Since life begins at conception (see preceding question) and God created us in His own image (Gen. 1:27), we believe it would be unethical to destroy life, even in the pursuit of medical research. Dr. Jacqueline Chadwick provides the following insight:

> Ethical codes have repeatedly stated that it is unethical to do human experimentation (Nuremberg Code, the Council of Europe's Convention on Human Rights, NIH guidelines for Human Research). Is it wrong to sacrifice one human being for the benefit of another, especially when that sacrificed one is in the most vulnerable state possible? If we say that this is acceptable, why would it be wrong to kill terminally ill patients to obtain their organs for transplant so that we can benefit all those hundreds of patients awaiting organs? There

is a tremendous moral difference between a human being dying of natural causes and someone killing them. We have no right to pursue good ends using unethical and immoral means (Dt. 27:25; Rom 3:8).[1]

---

[1]Dr. Jacqueline A. Chadwick, "What's the Big Deal? Human Embryonic Stem Cell and Cloning Research," *Leaders In A Changing World*, Fall 2001, Vol. 1, p. 4.

America and God

Q: *Many Christians (including prominent figures) have attributed the September 11, 2001 terrorist attacks on America as the "judgment of God." Could you state your position on this issue?*

A: The Bible does say in Psalm 33:12a, "Blessed is the nation whose God is the Lord," and in Proverbs 14:34 that "Righteousness exalts a nation, but sin is a disgrace to any people." Furthermore, it is true that God judges nations collectively (see Joshua & Judges). There are many great things about America, but we are, nevertheless, a nation that is infamous for pornography, abortion, etc. It is also true, as Habakkuk lamented (Hab. 1:12,13), that sometimes God utilizes the wicked in His acts of judgment.

However, we should proceed with the utmost caution in proclaiming such an event as 9/11/01 as an act of God's judgment rather than an act of evil committed by sinful men. We must remember that, unlike ancient Israel, the United States is not a theocratic government. Likewise, perhaps the only way to know with absolute certainty if such an event was God's judgment is if, like in ancient Israel, a prophet had provided a prophetic warning of impending judgment.

Q: *Where does the Bible talk about destruction of the World Trade Center?*

A: The Bible does not specifically predict the destruction of the World Trade Center.

Q: *Since Bible prophecy does not mention America, does this mean the United States will not be in existence during the end times?*

A: Not necessarily. The Bible does not specifically mention any nation in the entire western hemisphere. The absence of the United States, Canada, Mexico, Brazil, Argentina, etc., does not necessarily mean they are not in existence during the "end times."

Baptism

Q: I raised my daughter in the Catholic faith and recently she has become a born again Christian at another church (not SBC). However, the church she is going to now has told her that her baptism does not count. In your opinion, does it really matter?

A: I think it is a great statement of faith on behalf of the parents to dedicate a child to the Lord. Baptism, however, as described in the New Testament is for believers who have made a cognizant decision to place their faith in Christ for salvation and who are aware of the implications of being His follower (see Acts 2:41; 18:8). Thus, it is essential that baptism be a personal decision of the convert. An infant, child, or even an adult who does not understand God's plan of salvation through Jesus cannot make that kind of commitment.

The Scriptural example is to first believe and then be baptized, and as an ordinance is limited to those who have personally believed in Jesus as their Savior (Acts 10:47-48; Mt. 28:19). We are not baptized to obtain salvation (Eph. 2:8,9). Rather, we are baptized to publicly proclaim that we have already believed and received salvation in Jesus Christ (Acts 8:12; 16:33) and are now obediently following the teachings of Jesus.

Q: I have a four-year-old son. Should I get him baptized?

A: Baptism as described in the New Testament is for people who are fully cognizant of the implications and ramifications of becoming a follower of Jesus Christ. SBC baptizes believers following their conversion in order to demonstrate publicly their acknowledgement of Jesus Christ's transforming work in their lives. Therefore, although rare, if your four-year-old has had a conversion experience, yes, he is eligible for baptism.

Q: I work with a fellow Christian who recently began attending a Church of Christ church. He was recently baptized and has been pressing me to do so to ensure my salvation. I am born again but haven't yet been baptized. My friend is insistent that I need to be baptized in his church and by a Church of Christ minister in order to be saved. Could you please provide me with some biblical evidence that baptism (regardless of what church it is in) is not required for salvation?

A: The necessity of baptism for salvation is a position that simply cannot be correctly interpreted from Scripture or the teachings of Jesus Christ. It is most certainly an incorrect interpretation to hold. Such a view is in fact a works-based religion, which is in clear contrast to Ephesians 2:8,9, which reveals that salvation is solely through faith in Christ and not a work. Most evangelical churches correctly regard baptism as a command which all new Christians are expected to obey, but not as a requirement for salvation.

Of course, the classic passage that demonstrates that baptism is not necessary for salvation is the incident of the thief on the cross. Christ told the thief that he would be in "paradise," and yet he was never baptized (Lk. 23:43). My personal favorite is a passage from *The Message* (a dynamic equivalent translation), in which John the Baptist says to the Pharisees: "Brood of snakes! What do you think you're doing slithering down here to the river? Do you think a little water on your snakeskins is going to make any difference? It's your life that must change, not your skin!" (Mt. 3:7,8).

In addition to the thief on the cross, the New Testament records that some believers were saved before baptism. Cornelius and his family exhibited a filling of the Holy Spirit and a manifestation of the gifts of the Spirit after hearing the gospel but before being baptized (Acts 10:44-48). Therefore, it was not baptism that saved them, but their belief in Christ (Acts 10:43). Baptism is the public demonstration that a person has placed his or her faith in Christ and has become a follower of His teachings. It is an ordinance and a command, but it is not a prerequisite for salvation.

Baptism is an expected action of obedience for a follower of Christ

(Mt. 28:19,20). If you are a believer in Christ and have not been baptized yet, I would like to encourage you to contact our church office and attend one of our upcoming baptism classes. We would be delighted to provide you with the opportunity to show your friends and family, including your church family, that your faith is in Christ and you are one of His followers.

Q: I have been a member of the Roman Catholic Church my entire life (I'm twenty-five). My boyfriend is a member of your church. We have discussed marriage and frequently discuss the role of religion and faith in our lives. We believe it's important that we worship in the same church and raise children in the same faith community. My question is: What are the major differences between your church and the Catholic Church? What is the process of leaving one faith to join another? Obviously I've been baptized, but is that baptism recognized in all Christian faiths? I have to admit that I'm a bit sheltered when it comes to other denominations of Christianity. I've never considered joining another church until now. My boyfriend and I both believe that the Lord brought us together and, in return, we want to worship together. Your advice is greatly appreciated.

A: Thanks for the question. As always it is rather difficult to broad-brush an entire denomination, and so let me preface the following comment by stating it is a generalization. The most important issue with any faith is in the area of salvation. Biblically-based evangelical churches such as SBC emphasize that salvation is available strictly through the grace-based atonement of Jesus Christ (Jn. 3:16; Eph. 2:8,9). Some belief systems teach a non-biblical, works-based doctrine of salvation comprised of actions such as baptism, Eucharist, penance, last rites, etc.

With regard to leaving one faith to join another, I would highly recommend that you first attend the Class 100[1] series to learn the elementary tenets of Christianity that we believe and practice here at SBC. In addition, we practice believer's baptism in that we follow the

---

[1]Class 100 is a six-week course that covers the topics of Jesus, the Bible, prayer, assurance of salvation, understanding God's will for your life, and developing a personal testimony. For more information call 480.824-7334.

New Testament model of only baptizing those who have placed their faith exclusively in Jesus Christ for salvation and are aware of the implications of being a follower of Jesus Christ. Thus, if you have had a conversion experience in which you asked Christ to save you and were baptized thereafter, there would be no need for you to be baptized again. Nevertheless, we do offer a baptism class and you'd be welcome to attend it.

Finally, let me add that it is very wise of you to seek counsel regarding these issues prior to marriage, and I would also suggest you see one of our counselors for more individualized attention, or simply visit the church office during business hours and ask for a pastor. You may want to consider reading the book *The Gospel According to Rome* by James McCarthy to get a more detailed analysis of the similarities and differences between evangelical Protestantism and Roman Catholicism. Likewise, visit our outreach section on the website under *personal outreach training* to find out about the next Roman Catholic Roots class.

Q: What is the significance of baptism? Why do we practice it? What does it mean? How did it get started?

A: The earliest occurrence of baptism in the New Testament is with John the Baptist (Mk. 1:9-11; Mt. 3:1-17). However, we practice it today because Jesus commanded us to do so in His final instructions to His disciples (Mt. 28:19), and so we demonstrate our love for Christ by our obedience to His commands (Jn. 14:15). In Acts faith and repentance are the prerequisites for baptism (Acts 8:13), and according to Paul it represents the believers' union with Christ through a symbolic participation in the death, burial, and resurrection of Jesus (Rom. 6:4), and is a public celebration of their incorporation into the Body of Christ (1 Cor. 12:13).

4

Beauty

Q: What is the church's opinion on girls wanting to be so thin that it results in health-related problems?

A: Our bodies are created in the image of God (Gen. 1:27), and so it is our position that to deny the physical body necessary nourishment is poor stewardship of God's special creation (1 Cor. 3:16,17). God also expects us to utilize our common sense. Since we only get one body it is important that we take good care of it so we can be as resourceful as possible in modeling Christ-like behavior to non-believers. We are not to waste or despoil our bodies. Rather, we are to take good care of our bodies so that we can use them in service to God and humanity.

5

The Bible

Q: I have just finished reading the Old and New Testaments and the Koran. Many people say that all of these books are the word of God written by His prophets. Do you think this is correct? How do we know which so-called "sacred writings" are from God and which are not?

A: Unlike any other collection of sacred literature, the Old and New Testaments have the unique distinction of being supernaturally inspired by God (2 Tim. 3:16,17). The vast majority of the Old Testament was written or authorized by a prophet, whereas the New Testament has the same qualifier in that it had apostolic authority and authorship and was theologically congruent with the rest of Scripture. No other sacred literature meets these two qualifiers. Likewise, non-biblical writings contradict the historicity, congruency, and theology of the Old and New Testaments. Furthermore, with the Ascension of Jesus Christ and the completion of the book of Revelation the canon of Scripture is now completed.

Q: I have a friend that is driving me crazy with his suggestion that those who do not read the King James Bible are deceived. His reasoning is that "the King James language has not been changed as all other Bibles have." He likes to quote from Revelation 22:18-19. What can I say to put an end to his accusation?

A: The Bible was composed primarily in two languages. The Old Testament was written in Hebrew, with some Aramaic portions, and the New Testament was written in Greek, but translations were made into other languages quite early. Jerome translated Scripture into Latin in 410. The first English translation (*The Wycliffe Bible*) was made available in 1382. In the early 1600s King James I of England commissioned fifty-four scholars to undertake a newer translation that utilized the *Bishop's Bible, Tyndale's Bible,* and the Greek and Hebrew manuscripts available at the time. The translators completed the work in 1611. Thus the KJV is a translation.

Since 1611 our access to biblical manuscripts in the original Greek and Hebrew has increased dramatically. Most notable was the discovery of the Dead Sea Scrolls in 1947, which in addition to affirming our existing texts provided enhanced insight and understanding of the Bible.

Furthermore, we simply don't communicate the way they did in England at 1611. For example, Acts 28:13 says, "And from there we fetched a compass...." The Greek word *perielthontes* (Eng. tacking) was best translated as "fetch a compass" for the KJV, but today it is better translated as "we sailed around." The point being that English has changed since 1611 and the goal of an English version of the Bible is to simply provide the best translation possible.

There are three primary methods for translating Scripture. The first is called the concordant or literal method. This method is a pure word-for-word translation, in that the translators seek to stay as close as possible to the word order and grammatical forms of the Hebrew and Greek as they translate into the target language. The KJV, NKJV, and NASB are popular versions of this method. The second type is known as the dynamic equivalent method. Here, the primary goal of the translators is to transfer the *meaning* of the manuscripts into modern-day English without a slavish adherence to the word order and grammatical forms of the original Greek and Hebrew. The NIV and *The Message* are popular examples of this method. The third type is known as a paraphrase. This, of course, is a much looser method of translating that may or may not access the oldest manuscripts. *The Living Bible* is perhaps the best example of the paraphrastic method.

At SBC we use the NASB because as a Bible church we want to stay as close to the original form of the existing manuscripts as possible. Likewise, the English is contemporary enough not to confuse the average reader. From time to time in my personal use I may use the NIV or NKJV. I even served as a contributor to the NKJV *Nelson Study Bible.* If your friend has an open mind about the subject, one of the better books on this issue is *The King James Version Debate* by D. A. Carson. Alan Duthie's *How to Choose Your Bible Wisely* is also an excellent resource on translations in general. May God bless you as you continue to study His Word.

Q: While I enthusiastically study the Bible on my own, I am not at the point where I can gain the insight that I get when you present it. Do I need to study Hebrew and Greek or attend seminary? I want to be able to understand the deep meaning of the passage and be able to interpret it in light of other Scripture. How do I get to that point?

A: Thanks for asking. I'm encouraged by your desire to become a scholar of the Word. There are a number of excellent tools that can help you gain a deeper insight into the Bible, such as commentaries, word studies, and a good study Bible. Being able to read Greek and Hebrew is not a prerequisite for developing a deep understanding of the Bible, but it is a necessary ingredient for becoming a true scholar of Scripture. That is why nearly all of the Master of Divinity programs (M.Div.) in evangelical seminaries require an understanding of Greek and Hebrew. We are blessed to have Phoenix Seminary in our own backyard, and if possible, I would encourage you to take advantage of it. A working knowledge of the biblical languages provides insight into the Word that, on occasion, is not available in English.

Q: I know I need to be disciplined in reading my Bible, yet I find that I skip around a lot and I'm not sure which book to read first. Do you have any suggestions on how to study better?

A: For me, it has always worked best to read the Bible like any other book—from cover to cover. However, it seems that many Christians who adopt this approach get bogged down around Leviticus and give up. Therefore, I would recommend that you try starting with Matthew in the New Testament and focus on just trying to read through it one book at a time. Be sure to get a good study Bible that will tell you about the author, purpose of the book, etc.

Q: One of the most frequent criticisms I come across regarding the authority of the Bible is that at the Council of Trent a group of men decided what books should and should not be included in the Bible. Therefore, who is to say that these books that make up the Bible should be taken as the "sole representation" of Christianity, especially since scholars like Martin Luther disagreed on some inclusions, such as the book of James? Many people that I talk to in college claim that the Bible is nothing more than a non-objective source that fails to include other sources or books, which I must admit does not agree with anything in the Bible I've read. How do you explain this to those who see the Bible as something put together by men whose agenda was power over the masses rather than God's Word?

A: This is an excellent question. It seems to me that you are asking: What makes Scripture Scripture?

1.   It was written by a God-ordained prophet (OT), leader, or apostle (NT). In the Old Testament, these people were God-appointed and not self-appointed spokesmen or leaders for God's people (2 Pet. 1:20-21). This office is not one to which anyone would aspire because a prophet was expected to be completely accurate in his prophetic utterances, and if such accuracy were lacking it was grounds for execution of the prophet. In the NT, each of its authors were personally called by Jesus Christ to be a follower. (Paul meets this qualifier because of his Damascus Road experience). Thus in addition to being contemporaries of Jesus Christ, they were also personally selected by Him. In addition to this qualifier, they were also eyewitnesses to the risen Lord.

2.   It was confirmed internally. The Bible had been confirmed and in circulation long before the Council of Trent. This is confirmed internally by the New Testament itself (see, for example, Peter referring to Paul's work as Scripture, 2 Pet. 3:15,16) and also by the early second-century writings of Church leaders in which they refer to the books of the New Testament as Scripture (e.g., Clement of Rome).

3.   It was congruent with the rest of Scripture. Books that were not included in the canon of Scripture were those that were in direct contradiction to (1) the theology of the Old Testament prophets and (2) the apostolic teachings.

In regard to confirming the authenticity of the Bible, I like to borrow and customize the following easy-to-remember acronym from Hank Hanegraaff:[1]

M - MANUSCRIPT EVIDENCE:

In addition to its congruency, both the quality and the quantity of biblical manuscripts is overwhelming. For example, one of the most famous ancient manuscripts is the writings of Plato. However, we only have seven copies, the earliest of which is from the year A.D. 900, approximately 1,300 years after its authorship. By contrast, the New Testament was composed no later than A.D. 90, yet we have over 5,400 copies and fragments of biblical manuscripts, with the earliest fragment being from about A.D. 125.

A - ARCHAEOLOGICAL EVIDENCE:

Archaeology continues to confirm the people, places, and events of the Bible. Thus it is historically accurate. If it were inaccurate then there would be some concern as to whether or not it could be trusted for spiritual truths, but the fact is that you can actually go to Bethlehem, see Golgotha, visit the location of the Seven Churches of Revelation, etc. Likewise, there really was a race of Hittites, a King David, a Jewish Exodus, a King Nebuchadnezzar.

P - PROPHETIC EVIDENCE:

Only God can know and control the future. Perhaps the Bible's documented prophecies, especially from the Old Testament, are some of its most convincing material. The destruction of Tyre, the re-establishment of Israel, the crucifixion of the Messiah were all documented centuries prior to the events. In about 250 B.C. the Greek world in Alexandria, a city known at the time for its love of books and education, requested that the Old Testament Scriptures be translated from Hebrew into Greek in order that they could also read and learn from these Hebrew writings. This Greek translation of the Old Testament became known as the Septuagint and was in circulation possibly as early as 250 B.C. The New Testament is also filled with prophetic evidence, most notable would be that of the destruction of the Temple in A.D. 70, which prophecy was made by Jesus Christ over thirty years prior to the event.

I hope this helps some. You may want to further your study by reading *The Journey from Texts to Translations: The Origin and Development*

---

[1]Hank Hanegraaff, *The FACE that Demonstrates the Farce of Evolution* (Nashville: Word Publishing, 1998), "Appendix B—The Bible: Human or Divine," pp. 128-133.

of the Bible by Dr. Paul Wegner, *I'm Glad You Asked* by Ken Boa, and *The Case for Christ* (NT) by Lee Strobel.

Q: I'm really curious about the Hebrew Bible Codes and the factual evidence that the Bible is the inspired Word of God. Do you believe in this scientific finding?

A: Few Hebrew language scholars are taking the Bible codes very seriously because virtually anything can be read into it. Secondly, the codes are always interpreted *after*, not prior, to the events.

Q: What is your position on the TNIV Gender Bible?

A: Accurately translating and teaching the Scriptures is at the very core of our beliefs here at SBC. The most essential and elementary goal of translating the Bible into contemporary English is to remain as close as possible to the meaning of the original Hebrew and Greek texts. There are three primary theories for doing this. A concordant or literal version, such as the NASB, stays as close to the word order and grammatical forms as possible. The goal of a dynamic equivalent version, such as the NIV, is to translate the *meaning* of the original text into the target language. Both are acceptable methods of Bible translation. A paraphrase, such as *The Living Bible*, seeks to simply make the Bible as readable as possible, and may or may not even bother to consult ancient biblical texts.

Unfortunately, the TNIV employs none of the above. Rather, the recently-released *Today's New International Version* by Zondervan has intentionally mistranslated the texts, thereby distorting the original meaning of the Word of God. Here's just one of many examples:

HEBREWS 2:17

> For this reason he [Jesus] had to be made like his brothers in every way, in order that he might become a merciful and faithful high priest. (NIV)

> For this reason he had to be made like his brothers *and sisters* in every way, in order that he might become a merciful and faithful high priest. (TNIV)

First, the word in the Greek that is used is *adelphois*, which is the Greek term for "brothers." Therefore, it is an intentional mistranslation to include "sisters" because the term does not appear in the Greek text. Jesus was not like his sisters in every way. Thus, the TNIV lacks scholastic fidelity. Because of this and many other instances, the TNIV is not an accurate translation of the Word of God and appears to be guilty of outside political influence. Therefore, we do not consider it an accurate translation of God's revelation and thus cannot recommend it.

Q: I am a student at a local high school in Phoenix. One of my textbooks states that many of the stories in the Old Testament are not considered historical. Rather, it teaches that the Jews made up these stories to help them understand their faith. I was wondering what your stance is on the Old Testament and if you think it was mostly made up? Any help would be great.

A: In addition to being the inspired Word of God (2 Tim. 3:16), the Old Testament is also a trustworthy, reliable, and historical collection of manuscripts. Because the Old Testament, as well as the New Testament, refers to historical events, the Bible is verifiable and can be checked by external and historical evidence. There are many archaeological discoveries that illustrate the Old Testament's authenticity, but let me provide just a few.

Excavations of Nuzi (1925-41), Mari (1933), and Alalakh (1937-39, 1946-49) provide information that mirrors the environment, customs, and civilizations of the patriarchal period in Genesis. The Ras Shamra tablets shed light on Hebrew prose and poetry, and the Ebla tablets confirm the antiquity and accuracy of the Old Testament. Twentieth-century excavations also confirmed the account of Joshua's conquest of Canaan, etc.

Scholars have written entire books on how archaeology confirms biblical data. I would encourage you to get a copy of Dr. Paul Wegner's book entitled *The Journey from Texts to Translations: The Origin and Development of the Bible* and *Archaeology and the New Testament* by John McRay. Perhaps you could give one as a gift to your teacher.

Q: Why do Protestants and evangelical Christians have a problem with the

Apocrypha and the Septuagint, both of which the Catholics claim was the translation used by Jesus and the New Testament writers? Many Church councils approved and used the Apocrypha and Septuagint, e.g., the Council of Hippo in 393, the Council of Carthage in 397, Pope St. Innocent I in 405, and the Council of Trent in 1546. If the Church recognized the Septuagint for 1,100 years, why were the apocryphal books, which are in the Catholic Bible, disregarded at the time of the Reformation?

A: The Apocrypha is a great collection of inter-testamental and historical literature but it is very doubtful that it was regarded as Scripture by the vast majority of Jewish scribes and/or first-century Christians. The Jewish people in Jesus' day knew which books were in their canon, and Josephus lists them as twenty-two or twenty-four (these are the same ones we believe are in the Old Testament canon, only put together differently, e.g., the twelve minor prophets were considered only one book). Thus, the problem is not with the Septuagint, but with the canon that the early Church used and considered to be Scripture because it met very particular qualifications (see above). The apocryphal books do not satisfy these qualifications or criteria.

Indeed, Jesus makes the parameters of the Old Testament very clear in Luke 11:50-51 where He states that the Jews will be held responsible for the blood of the martyrs from Abel (Gen. 4) to Zechariah (2 Chron. 24:20-21). Genesis is the first book in the Hebrew Old Testament and Chronicles is the last book.

Q: I have been struggling for over a year to purchase a good study Bible. I know that I want NAS because that is what SBC uses. However, I am struggling with the original NAS versus the NASB. In Matthew 6:25-34, the NAS uses the word "anxious," whereas the NASB text uses the word "worried." Is there a significant difference between the two translations? I have looked seriously at the NASB Study Bible, the Ryrie NAS expanded edition, and the Life Application NAS Bible. What would be your recommendation?

A: We are glad that you have questions about what Bible to use. I believe the two Bible translations, NAS and NASB, are the same Bible. Sometimes different editions may change certain readings to clarify things, but basically they are the same Bible translation. If one of the versions of the NASB has changed the wording, it is because the editors think it captures the idea better. In this case (Mt. 6:24-25) they are trying to communicate the same idea. "Anxious" was probably the word they believed carried the significance a few years ago, but they seem to believe the more modern equivalent would be "worry." I know some of the people who have worked on the *Life Application NASB Study Bible* and it is pretty good at helping apply passages to our lives today. The others are good at supplying footnotes to help you understand the text better. The NAS and NASB are both good choices, but since you asked I would recommend the NASB.

Capital Punishment

Q: My Grandfather and I just had a discussion on capital punishment. Please explain to me again why capital punishment is accepted by God and what verses I can refer to when explaining it to my Grandfather.

A: The moral and biblical rationale lying behind the life-for-life mandate is based upon the Noahic covenant in Genesis 9, the Mosaic law, and the New Testament, which teaches that deliberately killing a human being created in the image of God can qualify one for capital punishment (see Mt. 5:38,39 with its context of Ex. 21:23,24). Christ objected to the misuse of this civil code for personal and private vengeance. However, the ethical directives of a life-for-life policy in the Old Testament for premeditated murderers is validated in the New Testament by statements from the apostle Paul with regard to the civil authorities (Rom. 13:4). These authorities exercise power derived from God and are under obligation to extend protection to society from violent criminals, which sometimes results in capital punishment.

Biblically, if government is performing its proper function for society, it will restrain by force those who are a violent and criminal threat to society. The implication of the Romans 13 text is that by failing to apply the sword as punishment the authorities "praise" evil and negate what is good. The death penalty is not an initiation of force as is murder; rather it is a response to violent force. Whereas private vengeance is prohibited in Romans 12, permission for the government to administer action in the form of a death penalty for murder follows in the immediate context.

Charismatic Gifts

Q: Why don't we see modern-day church leaders like you perform miracles, raise the dead, and speak in tongues as they did at Pentecost?

A: Pentecost was a one-time eschatological event. Its primary purpose was redemptive-historical and not experiential or normative. Thus, we should not expect the coming of the Holy Spirit at Pentecost to be any more of a repeatable event than Moses at Mt. Sinai or the resurrection. The miraculous gifts themselves (raising the dead, healing, tongues) seem largely confined to the apostles[1]themselves, and the apostles express no concern for other believers to acquire the miraculous gifts. Rather, they are encouraged to seek the more practical ones (1 Cor. 14:12).

2 Corinthians 12:13 at least suggests that certain gifts were related specifically to the apostles and that these particular gifts confirm them as God's messengers. (This was similarly the case with many of the Old Testament messengers or prophets, such as Moses and Elijah). Thus the miraculous gifts confirmed the authenticity of the apostle's message for introducing the gospel.

This is not to imply that God does not perform miracles today. He does. The question is whether believers are still gifted with "apostolic" gifts today and the evidence *seems* to indicate that it was a phenomenon of Pentecost and the apostolic age and not the norm for today (Eph. 2:20).

---

[1]An apostle was one who was a contemporary of Jesus Christ, witnessed the resurrected Christ, and was personally called by Jesus Christ to be a messenger and minister of the gospel. There are no apostles today.

Q: I am very confused about the gift of tongues. Do you believe that Christians should still practice the charismatic gifts of the Holy Spirit (tongues, etc.)?

A: There are disagreements and differences within Christianity about what are called the sign or charismatic gifts (e.g. healing, tongues, prophecy, and raising the dead). (See 1 Cor. 14:1-25.)

Before exploring the gift of tongues, we must remember that the Apostle Paul said the whole purpose of doctrine is love (1 Tim. 1:5). As disciples of Jesus, it is our love and respect for one another that makes us different from the rest of the world. Relationships in the world seem to depend on agreement. However, members of the family of God may disagree as a family. In the family of God, our relationships depend ultimately upon our faith in Jesus Christ as our Savior and Lord. Likewise, our alliance as brothers and sisters in Christ is far more important than whether we all reach the same conclusion on the issue of the gift of tongues. Therefore, we may disagree, but we disagree agreeably. Now with that in mind, let us look into the controversy over tongues, and at the same time learn of God's design for prophecy.

We become confused when we go beyond what is written, as was the case with the Corinthian believers.

> Now these things, brethren, I have figuratively applied to myself and Apollos for your sakes, that in us you might learn not to exceed what is written, in order that no one of you might become arrogant in behalf of one against the other (1 Cor. 4:6).

Experience as the standard is not always consistent, credible, or even true. It is very much a real part of all our lives and yet can conflict with itself or with the Scriptures. The Word of God is clear on what our standard is to be. "Be diligent to present yourself approved to God as a workman who does not need to be ashamed, handling accurately the word of truth" (2 Tim. 2:15; cf. 2 Tim. 3:16-17). The Corinthians had moved away from what was written and into their own experience as the test of truth. Thus they were left in divisive confusion.

In 1 Corinthians 12 Paul tells these believers of the spiritual gifts, and addresses the issue of the gift of tongues and the gift of prophecy. We shall see that the gift of tongues was the Spirit-given ability to speak a foreign language without ever learning it. It was a gift used in evangelism. It was also a sign to those who did not believe (not to those who did) to confirm the authenticity of the messenger. Prophecy, on the other hand, was the declaration of the revelation of God so that others (believers) could understand it and grow in their faith.

Paul's appeal to the Corinthians was for the edification of the body of believers in Christ, the building up of one another in faith. The Apostle ends the chapter with, "But earnestly desire the greater gifts. And I show you a still more excellent way" (1 Cor. 12:31). He desired them to know that love (i.e., the responding to one another with the worth and respect God has set upon each and every one of us) was more excellent in the sight of God than the pursuit of spiritual gifts.

Paul begins the fourteenth chapter, "Pursue love, yet desire earnestly spiritual gifts, but especially that you may prophesy" (1 Cor. 14:1). This pursuit of love means only one thing: the edification of the body of Christ, the Church. Paul sets the two gifts next to each other and probes as to which gives the greater manifestation of love for one another.

GOD'S DESIGN FOR THE GIFT OF PROPHECY

> Pursue love, yet desire earnestly spiritual gifts, but especially that you may prophesy. For one who speaks in a tongue does not speak to men, but to God; for no one understands, but in his spirit he speaks mysteries. But one who prophesies speaks to men for edification and exhortation and consolation. One who speaks in a tongue edifies himself; but one who prophesies edifies the church. Now I wish that you all spoke in tongues, but even more that you would prophesy; and greater is one who prophesies than one who speaks in tongues, unless he interprets, so that the church may receive edifying (1 Cor. 14:1-5).

To "pursue" means to chase after with intensity. In other words, if we are going to get intense about something, get intense about loving one another. One way of loving others is to "desire earnestly spiritual gifts." "Gifts" is the Greek word *pneumatika*, meaning the manifestation of the Holy Spirit through you to help other Christians grow in their faith.

> For this reason also, since the day we heard of it, we have not ceased to pray for you and to ask that you may be filled with the knowledge of His will in all spiritual wisdom and understanding, so that you may walk in a manner worthy of the Lord, to please Him in all respects,

bearing fruit in every good work and increasing in the knowledge of God; strengthened with all power, according to His glorious might, for the attaining of all steadfastness and patience; joyously giving thanks to the Father, who has qualified us to share in the inheritance of the saints in light (Col. 1:9-12; cf. 1 Pet. 2:1-3).

Our growth comes from understanding the will of God.

"All Scripture is inspired by God and profitable for teaching, for reproof, for correction, for training in righteousness; that the man of God may be adequate, equipped for every good work" (2 Tim. 3:16-17). To know the Word of God is to know and understand the revelation of God. Prophecy is the declaration of the revelation of God so that others can understand what God has said. If the revelation of God is being declared, young believers and non-believers will experience at least three things and probably four:

1. Sin: "And He, when He comes, will convict the world concerning sin, and righteousness, and judgment" (Jn. 16:8). The Word of God makes a man see he is a sinner. Thoreau, the naturalist, was asked by his aunt at the time of his death if he had made peace with God. His response was his answer, "I didn't know that we had ever quarreled." Too many, like Thoreau, are utterly indifferent to the fact they have sinned against God. Prophecy will first cause a man to understand his state before God.

2. Accountability: There will be a day when we will stand and give an account. The Word of God shows a man he must answer for what he has done. Lack of accountability is not unlike the snowflake that does not feel responsible for an avalanche, or the little fourth grader who told his teacher, "I don't want to scare you, but Dad said if someone's grades don't come up, someone is going to get a lickin'." We stand responsible.

3. Reflection:

For the word of God is living and active and sharper than any two-edged sword, and piercing as far as the division of soul and spirit, of both joints and marrow, and able to judge the thoughts and intentions of the heart. And there is no creature hidden from His sight, but all things are open and laid bare to the eyes of Him with whom we have to do (Heb. 4:12-13).

The Word of God forces a man to look at himself, his motives and intentions of the heart. Example: A little boy came running to his mother, declaring he measured 8 feet, 4 inches tall. She soon discovered he was using a six-inch ruler to measure his 4-foot, 2-inch frame! By what do we measure our lives? We can rationalize the secret intentions of our hearts until they are exposed to Scripture.

4.   Devotion: If a man is willing to repent, the Word of God brings him to his knees before the true God. "One who speaks in a tongue edifies himself; but one who prophesies edifies the church" (1 Cor. 14:4).

GOD'S DESIGN FOR THE GIFT OF TONGUES

There is no record that Jesus ever spoke in tongues. In searching the Scriptures, we find tongues are spoken of in only four places: Acts 2, on the Day of Pentecost; Acts 10 and 11, at the house of Cornelius; Acts 19, with John's disciples; and 1 Corinthians 12-14, speaking of the abuse of tongues in Corinth. (Some will mention Mark 16, yet the account cannot be found in the older and better manuscripts.)

Of all the references, only one gives a full description of the gift (Acts 2:1-13). Luke, as a historian, goes into great detail and is very careful to tell us exactly what happened on that day of Pentecost. As a close traveling companion of the Apostle, Luke knew what Paul meant by the term "tongues." They were previously unlearned foreign languages spoken with understanding. 1 Corinthians was written five years before the book of Acts; Luke was well aware of the contents of Paul's letter to the believers at Corinth.

"For one who speaks in a tongue does not speak to men, but to God; for no one understands, but in his spirit he speaks mysteries" (1 Cor. 14:2). The word *glossa* is used throughout Scripture for acknowledged languages. *Dialektos* (dialect), used in Acts 2:6,8, again speaks of known languages. "There are, perhaps, a great many kinds of languages in the world, and no kind is without meaning" (1 Cor. 14:10). *Hermeneuo* is the word for interpretation or translation of human languages. Therefore, if a language was spoken and no one could translate or understand what was being said, it was a "mystery" (that which is hidden) and only God could understand, for only God speaks all the languages.

> [H]ow shall we escape if we neglect so great a salvation? After it was
> at the first spoken through the Lord, it was confirmed to us by those

who heard, God also bearing witness with them, both by signs and wonders and by various miracles and by gifts of the Holy Spirit according to His own will (Heb. 2:3-4).

When the gospel first went out to evangelize the world, "signs, miracles, and wonders" accompanied it. In his first letter to the Corinthians, Paul states that one of these signs was the gift of tongues. Not everyone could speak the trade languages of Aramaic and Greek. However, the evangelist, with the gift of tongues, was able to communicate in a language and dialect he had never learned. Another unschooled individual, in turn, could interpret. The validity of the miracle came through the testimony of the unbeliever who witnessed this happening. They had heard the mighty deeds of God in their own language.

But what of the personal edification I would receive from speaking in tongues? In the context of 1 Corinthians 14, we need to see if personal edification is a good thing or bad. "But to each one is given the manifestation of the Spirit for the common good" (1 Cor. 12:7).

> Now I wish that you all spoke in tongues, but even more that you would prophesy; and greater is one who prophesies than one who speaks in tongues, unless he interprets, so that the church may receive edifying (1 Cor. 14:5).

Paul is not saying the gift of tongues, as God designed, is wrong but that the greater gift is to edify others—specifically the church. He has said that he wants us all to speak in tongues. Remember now that the word "wish" is the same as he used in 1 Corinthians 7:7 to wish we all were single. However, "All do not have gifts of healing, do they? All do not speak with tongues, do they? All do not interpret, do they?" (1 Cor. 12:30).

"So then tongues are for a sign, not to those who believe, but to unbelievers; but prophesy is for a sign, not to unbelievers, but to those who believe." (1 Cor. 14:22). Paul was making the point of building up the body of Christ. The gift of tongues was to be a "sign" for the unbeliever in bringing unbelievers to Christ. "But now, brethren, if I come to you speaking in tongues, what shall I profit you, unless I speak to you either by way of revelation or of knowledge or of prophecy or of teaching?" (1 Cor. 14:6). Paul states that without understanding, the gift of tongues is profitless. In contrast,

> Therefore let one who speaks in a tongue pray that he may interpret.
> For if I pray in a tongue, my spirit prays, but my mind is unfruitful.
> What is the outcome then? I shall pray with the spirit and I shall pray
> with the mind also; I shall sing with the spirit and I shall sing with the
> mind also. Otherwise if you bless in the spirit only, how will the one
> who fills the place of the ungifted say the 'Amen' at your giving of
> thanks, since he does not know what you are saying? For you are giving
> thanks well enough, but the other man is not edified. I thank God, I
> speak in tongues more than you all; however, in the church I desire to
> speak five works with my mind, that I may instruct others also, rather
> than ten thousand words in a tongue (1 Cor. 14:13-19).

Note again, the profitable use is when there is understanding.

Use Of Tongues (Without Understanding)

To further understand, we need a little background of Corinth. The temple built to the god Apollo was under the leadership of a priestess. She received messages from the gods and would speak to the people in ecstatic utterances. However, because no one could understand the gods except the priestess, she maintained tremendous power. Out of this situation arose confusion and abuse of the genuine gift of tongues in the church. Paul gives us three examples to show there is no profit nor edification of others if there is no understanding.

1.   "But now, brethren, if I come to you speaking in tongues, what shall I profit you, unless I speak to you either by way of revelation or of knowledge or of prophecy or of teaching?" (1 Cor. 14:6). Paul is stating his own case. His purpose is to share with them his "revelation" (receiving of the truth) to give them the "prophecy" and the "knowledge" to understand that prophecy, thereby teaching. If he were to speak to them in a language unknown to them and one they could not comprehend, it could not possibly benefit them.

2.   "Yet even lifeless things, either flute or harp, in producing a sound, if they do not produce a distinction in the tones, how will it be known what is played on the flute or on the harp? For if the bugle produces an indistinct sound, who will prepare himself for battle?" (1 Cor. 14:7-8). The Apostle gives an analogy with inanimate musical instruments. There must be a meaningful distinction in the sounds

emitted if music is to be distinguished from noise. The trumpet is not a signal unless it produces a sound that is recognizable.

"So also you, unless you utter by the tongue speech that is clear, how will it be known what is spoken? For you will be speaking into the air" (1 Cor. 14:9). "Speech that is clear" means easily understood so that others will comprehend what is being said and be edified, exhorted, and consoled (cf. 1 Cor. 14:3). If this is not accomplished, Paul says they will be speaking "into the air."

3.   "There are, perhaps, a great many kinds of languages in the world, and no kind is without meaning" (1 Cor. 14:10). Paul draws another comparison that was a frequent frustration among Corinthians. Corinth was a seaport and thus a commercial center. Encounters with foreigners were common, and although many spoke the trade languages of Aramaic and Greek, many could not. None of the languages were without meaning and it was the meaning that gave significance to the sounds that were spoken.

"If then I do not know the meaning of the language, I shall be to the one who speaks a barbarian, and the one who speaks will be a barbarian to me" (1 Cor. 14:11). In other words, if the meaning is not understood, we would become "barbarians" to one another. The Greeks would chide the non-Greek speaking foreigners about their meaningless sounds. The stuttering "bar-bar-bar" became *barbaros*.

"So also you, since you are zealous of spiritual gifts, seek to abound for the edification of the church" (1 Cor. 14:12). Paul's conclusion is that if the Corinthians are zealous for spiritual gifts, they needed to seek to build up others, not themselves (cf. 1 Cor. 12:7; 14:5).

Use Of Tongues (With Understanding)

"Therefore let one who speaks in a tongue pray that he may interpret. For if I pray in a tongue, my spirit prays, but my mind is unfruitful" (1 Cor. 14:13-14). If the gift is going to be profitable (edifying as a gift of the Spirit) and in the pursuit of love, there must be interpretation, translation, and understanding. Paul's reasoning is that if he prays in a tongue, his spirit and deep desires may be expressed but his mind is unfruitful. There is no understanding; thus there is no growth.

"What is the outcome then? I shall pray with the spirit and I shall pray with the mind also; I shall sing with the spirit and I shall sing with the mind also" (1 Cor. 14:15). Paul's conclusion is that when he prays with the deepest expression of his spirit, he prays with his mind also. He will understand what he is saying. When he sings expressing the deepest of feelings, he will sing with understanding (cf. John 4:24).

This next verse explains what he is saying, "Otherwise if you bless in the spirit only, how will the one who fills the place of the ungifted say the 'Amen' at your giving of thanks, since he does not know what you are saying?" (1 Cor. 14:16). Simply said, if they express themselves in a language no one understands, the ungifted or those who do not know the language will be unable to say "amen" (a Hebrew term of agreement). No one can agree to something he does not understand.

> For you are giving thanks well enough, but the other man is not edified. I thank God, I speak in tongues more than you all; however, in the church I desire to speak five words with my mind, that I may instruct others also, rather than ten thousand words in a tongue (1 Cor. 14:17-19).

The Apostle was not questioning their sincerity or motives, but the fact that there was no edification of others. God designed the gifts for building up others, not ourselves. "So also you, since you are zealous of spiritual gifts, seek to abound for the edification of the church" (1 Cor. 14:12). This verse sums up the fact that the design of the gifts and the pursuit of love demand we use our gifts to edify others, not ourselves.

Q: I'm confused. Why doesn't SBC practice and encourage the sign gifts like the book of Acts, Pentecost, and TBN? Aren't we all the same body of Christ? Aren't we supposed to strive to be like the church of Acts?

A: We believe that the Bible shows Pentecost to be a one-time historical event that we should not strive to repeat any more than we would the giving of the Law at Mt. Sinai, and similarly, that the events of Pentecost are not normative. Eschatologically, Luke (the author of Luke and Acts) shows that the message of Jesus reaches its climax in the baptism of the Holy Spirit with fire (cf. Lk. 7:18-28; 20:4; Acts 1:5; 2:32-33; 10:37). Likewise, Luke provides us with an eyewitness account of the apostolic ministry announced in Acts 1:8.

The use of the miraculous gifts provided apostolic authority specifically for the spreading of the gospel. In addition to being a contemporary of Jesus Christ, an apostle was one who was personally called by Jesus Christ Himself to be a believer and bear witness of His resurrection (Eph. 2:20). These sign gifts provided the evidence that the messenger indeed had the "signs of an an apostle" to authenticate their message (2 Cor. 12:12). The apostolic age ended in the early second century, and it is our belief that the sign or apostolic gifts ended with their deaths.

Q: What does the Bible teach about healing?

A: A theology of healing must first recognize that God is the exclusive Great Physician who is capable of preserving and restoring health. We should first pray to God for healing, and in particular cases it is appropriate to request the laying on of hands by the elders (Jam. 5:13-16). A miraculous healing is usually an instantaneous healing. When Jesus, for example, healed the man with leprosy, the cure was instantaneous (Mt. 8:3). Thus, a true miraculous healing by definition is a direct, instantaneous act of God.

Our Heavenly Father is grieved at the consequences that sin has brought upon His creation and nearly all the miracles that Jesus performed were snapshots of what the Kingdom of God would be like. Thus, we learn that in His Kingdom there will be no death, sickness, hunger, blindness, etc. (Rev. 21:4). However, it is also essential that we acknowledge that nowhere in Scripture is bodily health *promised* as a provision of salvation or faith. It is also noteworthy that not all sickness is the result of sin (Job 2:1-8; Dan. 8:27; Jn. 9:2,3).

Interestingly, in the ministry of Jesus faith was not explicitly demanded as a prerequisite for healing. In the few cases where faith was required, it was probably faith in Christ as the Messiah that was needed, not faith that the person could be healed. So, even in these cases faith *may* not be required in order to be healed, and in some cases it seems that Jesus performed miracles in spite of unbelief (see Mt. 17:14-21).

Although 1 Corinthians 12:9,30 refers to healing as a gift, it appears that it was one that most evangelical Bible scholars refer to as a "miraculous gift," which was limited to the apostles and apostolic era as an affirmation of the messenger and message (see 2 Cor. 12:12; Heb. 2:4; Eph. 2:20).

People who wanted healing brought their sick to Jesus and later to his apostles. James' instruction for elders to pray for the sick does not mention or indicate that any of these individuals actually possessed the gift of healing (Jam. 5:14-16). In fact, a check of a concordance reveals that apart from the mention of the gift of healing in 1 Corinthians 12:9 and praying for healing in James 5, the word "heal" is never used in the epistles (Paul's letters). This is in stark contrast to the numerous references to healing in the Gospels and Acts.

Nowhere else are the saints to minister to each other through the gift of healing, nor is it listed in the ministries of the church in 1 Corinthians 14:26. For the twenty-first century church to place an emphasis on miraculous physical healing or to hold special healing campaigns would therefore seem foreign to the first-century church (e.g., "By His stripes we are healed" mentioned by Peter, 1 Pet. 2:24, is in the context of the spiritual healing of our "souls," 1 Pet. 2:25).

8

Christmas

Q: Why do Christians celebrate Christmas on December 25?

A: It is true that the date of the winter solstice was at one time a pagan celebration to worship the sun. Secondly, it is true that December 25 most likely was not the date that Jesus was born. So, why do Christians celebrate it?

Why not?

We celebrate the birthdays of our friends and families, presidents and civil rights leaders, and so why wouldn't we want to celebrate the birth of Jesus—even if we do not know for certain the exact date of his birth?

The history of celebrating December 25 as the birth of Jesus is actually a testament to the creativity of ancient Christians who utilized the date to celebrate and worship the Son rather than the sun. As Christianity spread throughout the Roman Empire so did the "Celebration of the Son" on December 25. Today the party continues. For believers in Jesus, Christmas is a special time to reflect upon the uniqueness of the God-Man. In fact, it is a time when believers celebrate the deity of Christ.

And so, like the angels, adoring shepherds, and early believers, many of us use this season to take time out of our busy lives to celebrate the most important birth in the history of the universe. This Christmas may each of us pause to celebrate the fact that God offers a cure for sin and that He initiated spiritual peace to humanity through Jesus. "Glory to God in the highest, and on earth peace, goodwill toward men" (Lk. 2:14, NKJV).

Q: How should I prepare for the holiday season? Is there any Christian basis for Santa Claus, Christmas trees, and gift-giving?

A: Something happens to many people during this holiday time—a sensitivity to things they tend to ignore the rest of the year. There is no greater time, other than Easter, to touch people's lives with the gospel of Jesus Christ. With that, there come other stories that help us share the love of God with others:

SANTA CLAUS

Tell your children and others the story of Nicholas who began a ministry of delivering gifts to needy children in the name of Christ. Who is Santa Claus anyway? Take your children back to the very seed of where the tradition began. It began with a dear Christian man who loved God and loved children. In the fourth-century A.D., in the country of Lycia, which is present day Turkey, there was the Bishop of the city of Myra. His name was Nicholas, later called St. Nick. History tells us that he was a generous man who freely gave of his possessions to the needy, especially for the children. He died in 326, but the impact of this man's life was such that people remembered him, and that memory filtered out beyond the borders of Lycia.

The memory of this man has been twisted and merchandised almost to the point of absurdity. And yet, the testimony of this man's love and generosity need not be lost when we share the truth with our children of a man who lived many years ago and loved God and loved children.

CHRISTMAS TREES

You need not have one, but if you do share what it represents, high as hope and wide as love with a cross on every bough to symbolize the cross of Jesus that gave us life as an evergreen. Some tell us that Jeremiah warned us about decorating trees in our homes for a holiday (Jer. 10:1-4), but look at the context of the passage (vv. 5-8,11). We need to know what the Bible says, but also what it does *not* say. The context here has to do with idols of worship. If you are dropping to your knees and praying to your Christmas tree as a god, then you are practicing idolatry.

There have been many legends that have gathered around the origin of the Christmas tree, but it appears that the Christmas tree, as we know it, began in Germany. Tradition connects it with Saint Boniface, who came from England to preach Christ in the eighth century to the Germans. He cut down a sacred oak of theirs at Geismer, and on Christmas Eve, offered them a young fir tree in its place as a symbol of the new living faith he shared with them.

Decorating the tree can be traced back to Martin Luther who allegedly on one Christmas Eve was so amazed with the wonder of that starry night, cut a tree down and took it home to his children and decorated it with candles to represent the stars of that night and the wonder of creation.

By 1604 in Strassburg, Germany, the Christmas tree was an established custom. When Queen Victoria married Prince Albert, he introduced the custom into England. But even before that, German immigrants had brought the custom to America. The tradition of the Christmas tree is to give a symbol of the height of hope and the width of love given to us by God—a cross on every bough to remind us that it was the cross that brought hope and love; an evergreen, representing the enduring eternal life that our Savior brought to us that first advent.

GIVING GIFTS

Let them express your love and care. "I love you for He has loved me more!" If we give because Jesus gave, then we give as He gave. Our gifts are not to be tokens to appease the expectations of others, but rather are offerings of our love for one another and in honor of the Christ-child that was given gifts by the wise men. Good things have always been abused. But abuse ought not to be the reason we no longer do good things. Love is expressed by personal sacrifice. The greater care behind the gift the greater the love it communicates.

We Christians can love in season and out of season. Remember, gift-giving began with God Himself who gave us the gift of His Son. It is the nature of God to give. If we are children of God, it is our nature to do the same.

Q: *I have some friends who say we shouldn't celebrate Christmas because it was originally a pagan holiday. What do you say?*

A: I see it as a wonderful opportunity to share the gospel and to remind people of the uniqueness of Jesus Christ. It is a holiday that generally seems to cause people to be more sensitive and open to the teachings of Jesus Christ. Likewise, people seem to be more caring and sensitive to the needs of others during this season.

The history of celebrating December 25 as the birth of Jesus is actually a testament to the creativity of our spiritual ancestors who utilized the date by politely turning the tables on the holiday by worshipping and celebrating the Son rather than the sun. As Christianity spread throughout the Roman Empire, so did the celebration of the Son on December 25. And today people, non-believers included, take this date to revere and reflect on the incarnation (Lk. 2:11). So, like the angels and the adoring shepherds, we at SBC use this date and season to take time out of our busy lives to celebrate the most important birth in the history of the universe.

9

The Church

Q: Does the Bible specifically say we should gather in a building with other believers on Sunday to worship Him? Isn't it more important that we witness for Him, and have fellowship with believers and non-believers, anytime and anywhere? Even many believers think I am not a follower of Christ if I do not go to church every Sunday. In fact, isn't the term "church" misused because we, the believers, are actually the Church? I am struggling with guilt when I do not attend, but from my study of the Bible, I find that "wherever two or more are gathered, I am there," as Jesus said (paraphrased). I struggle with this due to my children, to whom I teach Christ and read the Bible. I do not want them to be part of a "religion." I want them to experience the Body of Christ all the time, everywhere.

A: You are correct. We should live every moment for Christ and not just on Sundays. However, to avoid church would be somewhat of an extremist viewpoint because as described in 1 Corinthians 12:12-27, we are meant to compliment one another, and together we can be a very powerful spiritual force. We, as a body of believers, miss out when we do not unite our gifts for service.

Meeting in a building is more for the sake of practicality. In Acts we are told that the first believers met wherever they could: temple courts, homes, openly, etc. Therefore, there is no prohibition against believers meeting in a building. In fact, it serves to help us coordinate our efforts, worship together as a community, partake in communion and baptism, and serve, encourage, comfort, and enrich one another.

Therefore, I would highly suggest that in addition to living a lifestyle of devotion to the teachings of Scripture that you gather with other believers here in the community to worship. I think it would be a disservice to those whom you are trying to disciple if you failed to encourage them to participate corporately.

It is also important to have some sort of spiritual accountability in our lives. Aside from the gospels, the bulk of the New Testament is addressed to first-century churches that congregated throughout the week and on Sundays to celebrate Christ's resurrection. Being a part of a church enables you to function under the guidance of spiritual mentors and elders for your edification as described in the New Testament (Heb. 10:23-25).

Q: According to the Bible, is there such a thing as a universal church that consists of all born-again believers?

A: Yes. Scripture says, "There are many members [individual people in the Church], but one body" (1 Cor. 12:20). This idea that all born-again believers form "one body" is repeatedly attested to in Scripture. Read the context of 1 Corinthians 12:20 (i.e., 12:12-27), paying special attention to the term "one body."

Ephesians 2:19 further explains this idea of a universal Church by stating that Christians are "members of the household of God" (NKJV). The verse does not say "households" (plural), nor does 1 Corinthians say "many bodies." There is one body, one household. See the context of Ephesians 2:19 (i.e., 2:11-22) in which Paul presents the oneness in Christ that we share as fellow believers.

Q: How do you address legalism in the church?

A: It is important that we agree on the essentials of the Christian faith (e.g., bodily resurrection of Jesus, [see Essential Christian Doctrine section]), but lifestyle regulations are often very subjective unless they are specifically addressed in the Bible. Attempting to enforce one's preferences as a spiritual barometer often results in legalism and bitterness. See, for example, how Paul responded in 1 Corinthians 4:1-5.

Q: Why does SBC only partake of the Lord's Supper once a month versus every week?

A: There has never been any question that the Lord's Supper is an ordinance and that we should practice it, but there is room for liberty in regard to the frequency of how often it is done. Some believers practice it daily, whereas others only once a year during Passover or Easter. It is true that after the resurrection the early church practiced it very frequently (Acts 2:42-46; 20:7). Nevertheless, there is no commandment from Christ or in the New Testament that we practice it daily, weekly, or even monthly.

Therefore, as long as we celebrate the Lord's Supper with some regularity and frequency, it is not an ethical issue. Since it is a very special time and one that shouldn't be taken lightly, we feel that it's best that the Lord's Supper be done periodically, rather than weekly or daily, in order that it not become redundant or ritualistic.

Q: If the Church began at Pentecost in Acts 2, then why did God need to raise up Paul to go to the Gentiles? Why didn't the disciples simply carry out the great commission and go into all the world with whatever gospel they were preaching—which they never did?

A: There is evidence that the apostles did do their best in taking the gospel to the uttermost parts of the earth. Thomas, for example, took the gospel into India where he was martyred. Eusebius tells us that Andrew took the gospel to Scythia; Peter preached the gospel in Rome to Jews and Gentiles; and Barnabas took the gospel to Cyprus (Acts 13 and 14).

In regard to Paul's specific calling, I cannot answer why God chose him to be the "apostle to the Gentiles," but thank God He did. His missionary zeal still inspires us today.

Q: My brother-in-law states that he is a Messianic Christian and insists that the "real" Sabbath is Saturday, not Sunday. He also keeps some Jewish laws, for example, not working after sunset on Friday, and he will not call Jesus "Jesus" but instead refers to Him by other names. He insists he is a Christian but I have shared with him that I do not think he understands the gift of grace God has given us as Christians. Do you know what a Messianic Christian is and are they correct in keeping some Jewish laws?

A: Yes, I have heard of Messianic Christians, and although we admire their desire to be biblical, it is unfortunate they do not realize the New

Testament clearly addressed these issues. However, if the Law were still in place, they would be bound to the entire Law and could not conveniently pick and choose which ones to practice as some Messianic Christians do.

The Old Testament Law reveals the moral character of God, and thus we would be unwise not to honor its principles. However, due to the death, burial, and resurrection of Jesus Christ we are no longer bound to them because Jesus Christ is the object of our faith. Thus, we are no longer under the Old Testament Law (see Gal. 3:25,26; 4:1-9). This is because the Law prefigured the redemption that was wrapped up in the person of Jesus Christ.

This issue was fought out in the book of Acts, where God clearly revealed that we are now under grace and not the Law (see Acts 11:1-9; 15:1-11). Please also refer your friend to Galatians 3:15-25, especially v. 25, "Now that faith has come, we are no longer under the supervision of the law" (NIV). Simply put, this means that the entire Mosaic Law comes to fulfillment in Christ and therefore we are no longer under its direct supervision. It is also noteworthy that it can be argued that many of the laws were specifically for the nation of Israel and some were for civil purposes.

We worship on Sundays and not Saturdays because Jesus Christ was resurrected on a Sunday. Matthew 28:1 is best translated as follows: "After the Sabbath, as the first light of the new week dawned...." In fact, all of the resurrection accounts verify this. In Mark 16:2 the Greek reads, "And very early on the first day of the week...." I assume that some of your friend's questions have to do with when the Sabbath begins and ends. Technically, the Sabbath ended at sunset on Saturday, thus confirming Sunday as the resurrection day.

The disciples and early church actually met daily (see Acts 2:42-47), but they had a special celebration on Sunday due to the resurrection. This is actually an incredible testimony to the authenticity of the resurrection because traditionally Jews met on Saturday. Changing the Sabbath day would be similar to someone changing the date for a cultural norm such as Christmas. Therefore, this radical departure indirectly testifies to the fact that something incredible occurred on Sunday—the resurrection.

For example, imagine you went away on vacation out of the country and when you came back you'd discovered that the dates of

Thanksgiving and Christmas had been changed virtually overnight. Since Jesus Christ was the fulfillment of the ceremonial laws we are no longer bound to the Old Testament Law, and therefore, to commemorate his resurrection, Christians for the most part still celebrate on Sundays. However, any day of the week would be fine (Rom. 14:1-10; Col. 2:16).

10

Cloning

Q: What wisdom from the Bible can we use to evaluate a position on cloning of humans or human embryos?

A: Cloning will become a more pressing issue in the next decade. Interestingly, it seems that most of the researchers are hoping that cloning technology will be a medical breakthrough that will help prevent various diseases, deformity, etc. With its current state it would be biblically unethical because embryonic research for cloning requires that most of the embryos be sacrificed in the name of research. Since life begins at conception (see the comments on Abortion) *current* cloning technology would be unethical.

11

Cremation

Q: What does the Bible say about cremation? I am in the process of revising my will and want to ensure that my requests are biblical.

A: The Bible does not speak specifically on cremation, and it is not a moral issue. Genesis 3 is very clear that we return to dust, and so regardless of burial methodology, we eventually return to the substance of our creation. Likewise, it will not be a problem for God to resurrect you if you should choose to be cremated.

On a strictly historical note, Christians were the first to be buried facing east, symbolic of the time in which we will be reunited with our bodies at the resurrection, similar to Christ's return. First-century Christians started this tradition based on Matthew 24:27 in anticipation of the Lord's return, "For just as the lightning comes from the east, and flashes even to the west, so shall the coming of the Son of Man be." Although this passage is not to be interpreted literally, this is the origin of the traditional Christian burial as we know it today. Therefore, in a very limited way, the Christian burial can serve as witness to your faith long after you have passed away.

12

Dating and Relationships

Q: I have been dating my boyfriend for over a year now, and we are very serious. We have been talking about marriage, and we hope to get married in two years or so. It is so hard to stay completely pure. Do you have any suggestions?

A: I admire your concern and desire to stay pure, and can assure you that you will be glad you did on your wedding day. Aside from praying at the beginning and end of each date, agree upon a few boundaries that will help keep you out of potentially tempting situations, such as (cf. 1 Thess. 4:1-8):

- Don't sleep over at each other's place.
- Don't sleep together.
- Avoid extended periods of kissing.
- Keep your clothes on.
- Avoid isolation. Double date. Get to know each other's in-laws and friends.
- Go on dates that will keep you in public, not private, arenas.
- Join a Bible study or enrichment hour.
- Get involved in a community outreach project.
- Pray.
- If necessary, get married sooner (1 Cor. 7:9).

Q: I am aware of the Scriptures on immorality (1Thess. 4), but a friend says he loves me and wants sexual pleasures, which I know is permissible in marriage only. He indicated that if we confess our sins or repent, premarital sex is justified. Isn't it true that such a lifestyle will result in God's punishment? He indicates God does not punish. I would appreciate any insight you can provide.

A: This would be a clear and obvious violation of God's design for intimacy. 1 Thessalonians 4:3,4 says, "It is God's will that you should be sanctified: that you should avoid sexual immorality; that each of you should learn to control his own body in a way that is holy and honorable" (NIV).

Likewise, Paul said in Romans 6:12-16,

> Therefore do not let sin reign in your mortal body so that you obey its
> evil desires. Do not offer the parts of your body to sin, as instruments
> of wickedness, but rather offer yourselves to God, as those who have
> been brought from death to life; and offer the parts of your body to
> him as instruments of righteousness. For sin shall not be your master,
> because you are not under law, but under grace. What then? Shall we
> sin because we are not under law but under grace? By no means! (NIV).

Furthermore, this kind of disobedience would make both of you eligible for God's discipline (see Heb. 12:5-11).

Q: Pastor Darryl, how far is too far? Where would you say the Bible draws the line? Where should we set our boundaries? I have heard that kissing should not be done, but I have also heard that anything is acceptable above the neck. Do you believe the Bible does not permit kissing, that anything below the neck is not acceptable, or something else? I would like to know what you think.

A: 1 Thessalonians 4:1-8 instructs us that it is God's will that we abstain from fornication, i.e., any sexual act that is not between a husband and wife. For singles, I think that kissing above the neck is fine as long as the hands also stay above the neck. However, I would caution against extended periods of kissing in which both passion and temptation will simultaneously increase. Kissing below the neck (unless it's the hand) is definitely off limits until you are married. Save yourself for your honeymoon. You will not regret doing it God's way.

Q: I'm starting to fall in love with a very nice man who is not yet a Christian. However, he treats me just as nice as many Christian guys I have dated. Some of my friends from church have told me that I'm not supposed to date a non-Christian. This sounds a bit holier-than-thou and self-righteous to me. I am praying for him and I have brought him to church. What do you suggest?

A: 2 Corinthians 6:14 tells us that we are not to be yoked together with unbelievers. This command applies to intimate personal relationships that can lead to marriage. Although there are a handful of positive examples, generally, "missionary dating" is a very unwise practice.

Although it may not presently be an issue, it has the potential to greatly retard your spiritual growth if you remain in an intimate relationship with a non-believer, because you cannot truly pray or worship together. Likewise, it may affect parenting methods as well if you marry (e.g., see the question in the Faith in the Family section which is very typical of the type of scenario we as pastors regularly encounter from Christians who marry non-believers). These are vital elements for a successful marriage as designed by God.

I think that you can express the importance of spirituality without coming across as condescending and I would advise that you only date born-again believers (cf. 1 Cor. 7:39).

Q: My eighteen-year-old daughter is planning to move in with her ex-boyfriend, but she swears they are just friends now and wouldn't have sex. I told her that I could not support her moving in with him because it was wrong. She asked why it was wrong, and off the top of my head the only verses that seemed to apply were "to avoid the very appearance of evil" and the part of the Lord's prayer that says, "do not lead us into temptation." Are there any other applicable verses? Do you have any suggestions in addition to prayer as to how to handle the situation?

A: There are several reasons why I would discourage the two of them from living together. First, the fact that they were in a previous relationship does increase the likelihood that their romantic feelings may be rekindled. If this does occur, they have placed themselves in a very tempting situation (see 1 Thess. 4:1-8).

Secondly, as a believer, she is a testimony to her friends and neighbors. I realize it's a cliché, but nevertheless it is true that in many ways we are the only Bible some people will ever read. As a result, many of their neighbors will not know their relationship is platonic. They will assume they are living together. Therefore, it is important that they remain above reproach and abstain from the appearance of evil. Although it is a qualification for an elder (1 Tim. 3:2), I believe it is equally desirable for all believers to have a good testimony among those who are outside the Christian faith (see 1 Pet. 2:9-12; 3:16).

Q: Biblically, do women have the right to get mad when men stare at their bodies, when they obviously dress to show it off in the first place?

A: Good question. *Biblically*, Jesus taught that lust is sinful behavior that Christians should avoid (Mt. 5:28). Therefore, in spite of their attire, we do not have a license to lust. Although it is unfortunate that some women do seem to lack discretion in the way they dress (see Prov. 11:22), they still have the right to feel uncomfortable by gawking spectators.

13

Demons

Q: What does the Bible say about demons? I am so confused by what is presented on Christian television channels. What is legitimate? What is not? Can Christians be demon-possessed? I need to be able to explain to a friend what the Bible teaches about this subject.

A: One of the facets of postmodernism is spiritual curiosity, which often leads to an increased interest in the paranormal. As a result, there is a plethora of sensationalized deliverance ministries that seek to exorcise demons out of born-again believers. There is no doubt that the Scriptures affirm the existence of demonic beings. In fact, I personally believe that Ephesians 6:12 is the most disbelieved verse in the Bible. Likewise, passages like Mark 5 demonstrate that demons are capable of taking complete control over the body and will of an individual.

Although it is true that a believer can be demon oppressed, the Scriptures are silent on the specific issue of whether or not a Christian can be demon possessed. However, logically it would seem implausible because John makes it clear that God indwells believers (14:16,17,23). 1 Corinthians 6:15,19 points out that our bodies are "members of Christ" and the "temple of the Holy Spirit." Therefore, although demons may oppress and influence Christians, they cannot possess them.

14

Essential Christian Doctrine

Q: I have heard you reference the term "essential Christian doctrine" on a number of occasions. What exactly is it?

A: Essential Christian doctrine is the set of beliefs that we consider non-negotiable, whereas nonessential Christian doctrine can be debated within the body of Christ. The following would be examples of non-negotiable, essential Christian doctrine:

- All Scripture, both Old and New Testaments, was inspired by God, and thus is without error in the original autographs, and that as God's revelation, the Bible serves as the final authority on issues of faith and life (Deut. 6:4-9; Isa. 40:8; 2 Tim. 3:16; 2 Pet. 1:20,21).
- Jesus Christ was conceived by the Holy Spirit and born of the Virgin Mary, and He is both true God and true man (Isa. 7:14; Mt. 1:18-25; Lk. 1:31,35; Jn. 1:1,14; Col. 2:9).
- There is one God, eternally and simultaneously existing in three persons: Father, Son, and Holy Spirit (Deut. 6:4; Mt. 3:16-17; 28:19; Jn. 1:1,14; Acts 5:3,4).
- Salvation is by God's grace, through faith in the substitutionary sacrifice of Jesus for our sins, which results in God declaring the believer righteous, and this salvation is exclusively through Jesus Christ (Jn. 3:16; Acts 4:12; Rom. 3:23-28; 5:1; 10:13; Eph. 2:8,9).
- Jesus Christ was raised from the dead in bodily form, ascended to heaven, and is now seated at the right hand of the Father where He represents believers today as High Priest and Advocate (Mt. 28:5-9; Mk. 16:6-14; Lk. 24:36-43; Jn. 20:26-29; Acts 1:9-11; 1 Cor. 15:3-8; Heb. 4:14; 8:1; 1 Jn. 2:1).

- Jesus Christ will come again for His Church (Mk. 8:38; Acts 1:11; 1 Thess. 3:13; 4:16,17; 2 Thess. 2:1; Rev. 1:7).
- Mankind was created in the image of God, but sinned and thereby incurred not only physical death, but also spiritual death, which is separation from God; and that all human beings are born with a sinful nature, and in the case of those who reach moral responsibility, are sinners in thought, word, and deed in need of redemption through Jesus Christ (Gen. 1:26,27; Ps. 51:5; Rom. 3:10,23; 5:12; 6:23).
- God is the Creator and Sustainer of the universe and humanity (Gen 1-2; Jn. 1:3; Col. 1:16,17).

We would consider a deviation from any of the above essential doctrines to be heretical.

An example of nonessential doctrine would be the time of Jesus' Second Coming. While it is essential to believe that He is going to return, the specifics of when (before the tribulation period, during, or after) can be debated. At SBC, for example, we believe in the pre-millennial and imminent return of Jesus. In contrast, both of my sons (John and Kent) believe that Jesus will return after the Great Tribulation. Another example would be the age of the earth. Some, such as Dr. Walt Brown, believe in a young earth, whereas other Christians, such as Hugh Ross, believe in a very old earth. However, both believe that God created humanity and the universe, and neither believes in evolution.

Nonessential Christian doctrine can provide very stimulating study, discussions, and intellectual pursuits within Christianity. However, while they can be fun to debate, we should never divide over them.

15

Faith in the Family

Q: I have been married for 20 years. I became a Christian shortly after marrying. My spouse is still not a believer. I did the best I could in raising my children in the church. They are now teens and seem to be following in their father's unbelief. As a Christian mother, how much should I force my fourteen- and eighteen-year-old teens to go to church and be active in youth group?

A: I'm sorry to hear about your dilemma and know that it must be very stressful. However, since you appear to be the primary source of spiritual truth in your home, it is perhaps more important than ever before that you get spiritually nourished each Sunday by fellowshipping with other believers, worshipping, and learning from God's Word.

As far as your children go, I would encourage you to "invite" them to join you and/or participate with our Student Ministries while you attend a worship service or enrichment hour. The teen years are very formative years and they will need to be well-immersed in the Christian worldview prior to entering college, but you cannot force them against their will to embrace the teachings of Jesus Christ. However, your example will speak volumes in your ability to influence them (see 1 Cor. 7:14).

16

Forgiveness

Q: Can we forgive a non-believer who does not ask for our forgiveness? I notice that Jesus asked the Father, "Forgive them, for they know not what they do," even though they themselves did not ask Jesus for forgiveness.

A: Those who put Jesus to death acted in ignorance, not really understanding whom they were killing. Jesus asked the Father to forgive them for the particular act of crucifying Him and not for all of their sins. Stephen makes a similar request in Acts 7:60, when after being stoned he said, "Lord, do not charge them with this sin" (NKJV). In regard to whether a person can forgive a non-Christian for unconfessed sins, yes, it is possible, but complete reconciliation cannot take place until the offender acknowledges their wrong and then asks forgiveness.

In other words, we can only offer forgiveness if asked (see Lk. 17:4). However, we are still to love the person even if they do not ask forgiveness (Eph. 4:31; Rom. 12:17-21). In the Lord's Prayer of Luke 11 we are instructed to pray, "And forgive us our sins, for we also forgive everyone who is indebted to us" (Lk. 11:4a). Here, the petitioner recognizes that if mercy is to be sought from God, then mercy must also be shown to others.

Q: If my father who abused me as a child were to accept Christ and follow Him, would God forgive him for all that he did to me and would he be free from all of those consequences?

A: Yes, if your father accepted Christ as his Savior he would at that moment be declared forgiven of all his sins (2 Cor. 5:17-21; cf. 1 Jn 1:9): past, present, and future. Theologians call this justification. Similarly, the sanctification process would then begin in which he would begin to "Grow to be like Him."

Would he be free of the consequences? This is a much harder question for me to answer because it depends on a variety of circumstances, but no, not necessarily. It is somewhat like a man jumping off a bridge and then realizing he made a mistake and asking for forgiveness on the way down. He would be forgiven but would still face the ramifications of the decision by hitting the water below and possibly incurring injury or death. Nevertheless, I have seen a few cases in which God supernaturally intervened and rescued a person from the consequences, but this is, in my experience, rarely the case.

Finally, I would like to encourage you to contact our Biblical Counseling Center if you have never received counsel for the abuse and pain you experienced as a child.

Q: After we are saved are we required to ask God for forgiveness when we sin? Some people tell me that I am forgiven at salvation but lose fellowship with God when I sin and must ask for forgiveness to restore the fellowship. I have looked but I cannot find a passage in Scripture that talks specifically about fellowship forgiveness. Can you provide me with such a passage?

A: It is true that at the moment of salvation we are forgiven of all sins—past, present, and future (Jn. 3:16). At that point, we are declared righteous in that Christ's death, burial, and resurrection atones for our sins (Eph. 2:8,9). This is called justification. Sanctification is the ongoing process in the believer's life on earth in which he or she is being conformed to the image of Christ on a daily basis (2 Cor. 3:17,18). Sin does estrange us from God. Although we have been justified, we must still confess our sins so we will not quench the work of the Holy Spirit in our lives (1 Jn. 1:9). Likewise, an ongoing pattern of sin in one's life will result in God's chastisement (Heb. 12:7-11).

17

Genesis

Q: Who or what exactly are the "sons of God" in Genesis 6? My best interpretation is that they are fallen angels, but that interpretation seems like Greek mythology. I am confused. Could you help me out?

A: The passage involves cohabitation or intermarriage, which is not possible between fallen angels and humans (cf. Mk. 12:25). Genesis 6:1-4 is best understood as depicting people from the line of Seth who in the context of the ancient Near East would have been understood as the "sons of god." Up until this time in history, the descendants of Seth were the moral polar-opposites of Cain. Cain's descendants were infamous for proliferating wickedness. They introduced murder and polygamy. Apparently, prior to Genesis 6:1 they were also somewhat segregated from each other, but in Genesis 6:2 they began to intermarry, and it appears that this resulted in corruption within the line of Seth.

The ancient Aramaic Targums, for example, translate "sons of God" as "sons of nobles." In Genesis 6:4 the root meaning of the association between "Nephilim" and "gibborim" is a reference to a "mighty man of valor and strength, wealth or power." Nimrod, in Genesis 10:8, for example, was such a *gibbor*. He was also a king in the land of Shinar. Therefore, the best rendering in contemporary English for "sons of God" in Genesis 6 is "princes" or "great men."

Q: Since God knows everything, why did He create Satan? He knew the hell He would cause upon the earth.

A: God created both Satan and mankind with the freedom to choose. This freedom necessitates that we have the ability to make both right and wrong choices. A lack of choice would essentially result in a race of mindless robots. As the book of Job demonstrates, God desires that we worship and follow Him simply for who He is, but to force this upon His creation would be against His will and make Him somewhat of a cosmic dictator.

Q: My eight-year-old son asked me, "If in the beginning, God created everything, then who created God? Where did God come from?" When I responded, "God was just there," he asked, "How? How was He there?"

A: You have a very astute eight-year-old. It is sometimes difficult for our finite, three-pound brains to totally comprehend all there is to God, but perhaps it would help if you explained that God is eternal, which means that He has no beginning nor will He ever have an end. God is what some philosophers would call the uncaused first cause. Although everything else had a beginning, God has always been in existence (Ps. 90:2). Likewise, God is the Creator of time as we know it. In fact, He didn't even create the solar system, our way of measuring time, until the fourth day (Gen. 1:14-19).

Q: Why did so many Old Testament figures practice polygamy?

A: Interestingly, the practice of polygamy was first introduced through the line of Cain (Gen. 4:19). However, because the ancient Near East was an agrarian society many within it felt dependant upon establishing large families. Polygamy, although practiced by some Bible personalities, was never condoned by God. Indeed, in most cases polygamy resulted in domestic turmoil. God's plan is for monogamy, one man and one woman married for life (Gen. 2:18-24; Mt. 19:4-6).

Q: Did Adam and Eve have belly buttons?

A: I don't know, but since they were created directly by God and never in a womb, probably not.

Q: Is it possible that maybe God chose to use evolution?

A: There are people who believe in both God and evolution. This position is known as "theistic evolution." However, such a position contradicts the Bible because the Genesis account makes it very clear that God was the direct creator of Adam and Eve (Gen. 1:26,27; 2:7,22-25) as well as the animal kingdom (Gen. 1:20-28). There is absolutely no biblical support to even hint at evolution.

Scientifically, there are also a number of problems with evolution, such as an absence of fossil evidence to demonstrate the transformation of one species into another. Philosophically, it appears that planet earth has been created specifically with humanity in mind. For example, we are just the right distance from the sun—if it were any closer we would burn, and yet if it were farther we would freeze. Our moon is just the right size—if it were larger we would have massive flooding, and yet if it were smaller the oceans would stagnate.

If you would like to study this further please consult *In the Beginning* (7th edition) by Dr. Walt Brown and *The FACE that Demonstrates the Farce of Evolution* by Hank Hanegraaff.

Q: Why doesn't the Bible talk about dinosaurs?

A: Actually the Bible does talk about dinosaurs both directly and indirectly. Indirectly, we know that God is their creator (Gen. 1:20-25). Job appears to make direct reference to two types of dinosaurs in his description of behemoth and Leviathan, which *may* have been a brontosaurus and plesiosaur respectively (Job 40:15-24; 41:1-10).

Q: Where did Cain get a wife?

A: In Genesis 4:14 Cain implies that many others are living on the earth. Genesis 5:4 says, "After he begot Seth, the days of Adam were 800 years and he had sons and daughters" (NKJV). Since Adam and Eve were the first family, Cain *possibly* may have married a niece but most likely he married one of his sisters. The Bible does not tell us everything about the first family, or how old Cain was when he killed Abel, but a sister would be the most likely answer.

In many patriarchal accounts we are only provided with information on the son, but it was not uncommon for patriarchal families to have nine children or less. Dr. Walter Brown says, "If 10 or more children per family were typical before the flood, and plagues, famines, and wars were no more common than in the last several thousand years, then the world's population at the time of the flood would have exceeded today's population of 6 billion people."[1]

Q: What order did the dinosaurs, wooly mammoth, cavemen, and Adam and Eve come in? How do you explain the fossil records for these prehistoric creatures?

A: The short answer is that all forms of life and everything in the universe were created during the six-day Creation Week (Gen. 1; Ex. 20:11). Yes, man and dinosaurs lived at the same time. In fact it is very probable that Job was describing dinosaurs in Job 40:15 to 41:34 in his description of the Behemoth and Leviathan. Some believe that it is possible that many of the ancient depictions of dragons were inspired by dinosaur encounters.

Almost all fossils, including those of dinosaurs and mammoths, were formed during Noah's flood. Vast amounts of sediments were eroded by the subterranean waters that burst out of the earth, "the fountains of the great deep" (Gen. 7:11). As those sediments settled, they trapped and buried plants and animals, forming fossils.

The long answer to your question, along with much scientific evidence not in most textbooks, can be found in Walt Brown's book *In the Beginning: Compelling Evidence for Creation and the Flood* (7th edition). It is available at Scottsdale Bible Church's bookstore and it is on the website www.creationscience.com.

---

[1]Walt Brown, *In the Beginning: Compelling Evidence for Creation and the Flood*, 7th edition (Phoenix, Arizona: Center for Scientific Creation, 2001), p. 273.

18

Halloween

Q: Should Christians participate in Halloween?

A: There is no doubt that Halloween has some occultic origins. The jack-o-lantern, for example, is based on the legend of a man named Jack O'Latern who, because of his cunning dealings with the devil to escape hell, is allowed to roam the earth carrying a hollowed-out rutabaga containing a coal given by the devil. Other cultures falsely believed it was a night when, unlike any other, the dead and demons walked the earth, and thus people wore masks in the hope they would not be recognized if these evil spirits attempted to place a curse upon them.

However, you might be surprised to know that the word "Halloween" is actually a contraction of the words "Holy Evening," in reference to the evening before All Saints Day (November 1) when Christians remember believers who were persecuted and tortured for their faith rather than renounce Christ. Halloween became an American celebration in the late nineteenth century when immigrants from Europe and Britain began practicing their own unique version of it, incognizant of either its occultic *or* Christian roots.

Most American Protestants, who constituted the vast majority of European immigrants, stopped observing Halloween and All Saints Day due to the holidays' association with Roman Catholicism. Interestingly, Martin Luther chose November 1, 1517, as the date to publicly charge the church with abandoning essential Christian doctrine; and in many circles, November 1 is known as "Reformation Day."

The issue, as you have alluded to, is what should a Christian do on October 31? First, let me say that there is nothing magical about the date itself. Psalm 118:24 declares, "This is the day which the Lord has made; Let us rejoice and be glad in it." This includes October 31. God is sovereign over it as much as He is any other date. His omnipotence is neither weakened nor threatened by Halloween. Therefore, we do not have to go into our basements and hide, nor are we to engage in any occultic practices. You can respond to Halloween in three ways.

1. Unlimited Participation. As your pastor I would discourage unlimited participation due to the occultic aspects of many of the traditions, as well as the fact that our society is becoming less safe.

2. Abstinence. You can choose simply to have no involvement with it whatsoever. If it is not done in a condescending or judgmental manner, it is perfectly acceptable to refuse to participate in its customs or activities.

3. Moderate Participation. Many Christians choose to avoid the occultic trappings and yet creatively utilize the date as an opportunity to share the gospel and connect with their neighbors and community.

In fact, the history of utilizing December 25 as a date to celebrate the birth of Christ is a testimony to the creative possibilities of this option. Wouldn't it be a great legacy to leave to future Christian generations if we could begin to lay the groundwork for October 31 to be thought of as a day to reclaim the aspects of All Saints Day and Reformation Day through community celebrations that included the gospel?

At SBC, for example, we have had Harvest Festivals in which we invite our surrounding community to visit our campus for a night of good, clean fun and gospel presentations. Some Christians choose to stay home and provide candy *and* gospel tracts that are geared toward children to anyone who rings their doorbell.

Regardless of the option you choose, we would never ask you to sin against your conscience (Rom. 14:21). If you should choose the thirdoption, we ask that you strive to do it "to the glory of God" (1 Cor. 10:31).

19

Heaven

Q: Is there going to be a judgment for Christians, even though we are saved and going to heaven, or is the judgment only for those who never accepted Christ?

A: The Bible refers to the judgment of Christians as the "judgment seat of Christ" or *bema*-seat judgment (2 Cor. 5:10). This will be an opportunity to see how we utilized our gifts, talents, and lives for God's glory on earth (see Rom. 14:10-12; 1 Cor. 3:12-15). The great white throne judgment is for unbelievers (Rev. 20:11-15). Our sin has clearly been judged at the cross (2 Cor. 5:21). Therefore Paul says in Romans 8:1, "There is no condemnation for those in Christ."

Q: Will we know each other in heaven?

A: I think that we will. Although they did not recognize Him at first, the disciples on the road to Emmaus recognized Jesus (Lk. 24:13-35). At the transfiguration Moses and Elijah were recognizable (Mt. 17:3-4) and the rich man was able to recognize Lazurus in the afterlife (Lk. 16:23).

Q: Will our pets be with us in heaven? Is there any Scripture to comfort me in the death of my pet dog? It's been hard and painful because he was a loving fixture in my life for such a long time.

A: I am sorry to hear about your loss. Rest assured that God was pleased with how you cared for your pet. Proverbs 12:10a says, "A righteous man has regard for the life of his animal." As God's servants we are to be good stewards of His creation (Gen. 1:28). From the sound of things, unlike many animals, I am sure your pet was happy to be under your care.

We know that God delights in the creation of his animal kingdom (Gen. 1:24-25) and that they have a place in his millennial kingdom (see Isa. 11:6-9). Animals will probably be present in the creation of the new heaven and earth as well (Rev. 21:1). Biblically, there is no evidence to overwhelmingly confirm that our pets will be with us in heaven, nor are there any verses to say that they will not be present. However, it certainly wouldn't surprise me if they are there (cf. Eccl. 3:21).

Q: Where is heaven?

A: The Bible does not provide a geographical location of heaven. Paul speaks of the "third heaven" in 2 Corinthians 12:2. Some believe, therefore, heaven is out beyond the edges of the universe. Most likely it is in another dimension and thus it is more of a state rather than locale. The most important thing about heaven is that it is the final state for all born-again Christians.

Q: When we get to heaven will we instantly know everything?

A: Only God is omniscient. Therefore, although we will no doubt have a much higher level of intelligence in a body that is free from the effects of sin, and enjoy the community of all saints, I believe that we will be forever learning (cf. 1 Cor. 13:12).

20

Hell

Q: Do Christians really believe in a place called hell?

A: The New Testament uses three different words for hell: *Hades, Tartaros,* and *Gehenna.* By far, the most definitive term in the New Testament for hell is *gehenna* and Jesus referred to it more than anyone else in the Bible (e.g., Mt. 5:22; 10:28). Therefore, Christians who believe in the Bible believe in hell because the Bible describes it as the final state of those who never accept Christ as Savior (Mt. 25:41; Rev. 20:13-15).

Q: Do you believe that the "fires of hell" are literal or is the Bible just being metaphorical?

A: Both positions (literal and metaphorical) are acceptable and debatable within orthodox Christian theology; but since you asked, I personally believe they are literal. My literal view is largely based upon my belief that the account of Lazarus and the Rich Man in Luke 16:19-31 is not a parable but a true event. Regardless, even if the descriptions of hell provided in the Bible are metaphorical it is still a place of nightmarish proportions.

21

Homosexuality

Q: What does the Bible say about homosexuality?

A: In the Old Testament we find heterosexuality to be proclaimed as God's natural order of creation (Gen. 1:27; 2:18,22-24; 4:1). This was a teaching Jesus upheld in the New Testament. Biblically, the act of sodomy is described as both an "abomination" and "unnatural." God calls us to reject sin, but to love and value all people.

GENESIS 1-2

For those who believe that statements of the Bible are normative for our daily lives, the most important question to consider regarding homosexuality is: What was God's purpose in creating human sexuality? The answer to this question is more important than any other area of discussion. Simply put, sexuality is to be reserved for a husband and wife, and we could easily close the question with that answer. However, since this question regularly comes up it is important that we understand God's revelation to us on this topic.

From the very beginning of his revelation to humankind, God has revealed His order of creation, especially as it relates to sexuality. In Genesis 1 we are told that one purpose in creating the two sexes was procreative. Through the sexual union of male and female, we can reproduce the race: "Male and female He created them. Then God blessed them, and God said to them, 'Be fruitful and multiply; fill the earth and subdue it'" (Gen. 1:27b-28, NKJV).

In Genesis 2 we are provided with additional details that reveal that aside from procreation there is a function of heterosexuality that fulfills our need for companionship: "And the Lord God said, 'It is not good that man should be alone; I will make him a helper comparable to him'" (Gen. 2:18, NKJV). Then, after God created Eve and presented her to Adam, Adam rejoiced in his God-given companion. The chapter concludes: "Therefore a man shall leave his father and mother and be joined to his wife, and they shall become one flesh" (Gen. 2:24-25, NKJV).

In Genesis 2 several items emerge. First, man has need for companionship: "It is not good that man should be alone" (Gen. 2:18, NKJV). Second, God makes provision to meet this need: the creation of woman (Gen. 2:19-23). It is in Eve, a woman, that Adam, a man, finds completion. Third, God ordains the institution of marriage. We are told that the man would (1) "leave his father and mother," (2) "cleave to his wife," and (3) "become one flesh." Thus we find that heterosexuality is proclaimed to be God's natural order of creation and it is only in the heterosexual union of marriage that we find the fulfillment of God's intended order, both procreative and unitive.

Leviticus 18 and 20

One of the aspects of the Old Testament laws is that they reveal the moral character of God. Interestingly, many also served to protect humanity from self-destruction. Homosexuality is not permissible according to God's revelation. "You shall not lie with a male as with a woman. It is an abomination" (Lev. 18:22, NKJV). "If a man lies with a male as he lies with a woman, both of them have committed an abomination. They shall surely be put to death" (Lev. 20:13, NKJV). Other moral prohibitions listed in Leviticus include incest and adultery (Lev. 18:6ff; 20:10).

New Testament

In the New Testament, whenever the subject of sexuality comes up, the heterosexual norm of marriage is always upheld. For example, Jesus, in answer to a question, quoted Genesis 1 and 2:

> Have you not read, that He who made them at the beginning "made them male and female," and said, "For this reason a man shall leave his father and mother and be joined to his wife, and the two shall become one flesh"? So then, they are no longer two but one flesh. Therefore what God has joined together, let not man separate (Mt. 19:4-6, NKJV).

In addition, the apostle Paul reaffirms the norm of heterosexuality in several of his letters, in which he also quotes from the Genesis passages (e.g., Eph. 5:25-33; cf. 1 Cor. 7:2-3,10-16; 1 Tim. 3:2,12).

ROMANS 1:18-27

> For this reason God gave them over to degrading passions; for their women exchanged the natural function for that which is unnatural, and in the same way also the men abandoned the natural function of the woman and burned in their desire toward one another, men with men committing indecent acts and receiving in their own persons the due penalty of their error (Rom. 1:26-27).

In Paul's words, the homosexual is "without excuse" (Rom. 1:20). This initially sounds a bit harsh, but Paul's intent in Romans 1 - 3 is to show that all have sinned, Jew and Gentile alike, and turned from God. It is not an accident that the Apostle begins his argument with a reference to the Creator and His creation (Rom. 1:18-20). His Jewish/ Christian audience would immediately have connected this with Genesis 1 - 2, which, as we have seen, tells us not only about God's created order, but also about the complementary design of male and female within that order.

In his catalogue of sins in Romans 1:18-32, Paul lists homosexuality and lesbianism immediately after idolatry, not because they are the most serious sins, but because they are warning signs that a violation of reason and nature has occurred. Men have inverted God's order by worshipping the creature rather than the Creator, and as a signal of this error, like the blinking red light on the dashboard of a car which is functioning improperly, God has given them up to "dishonorable desires" in the inversion of their sexual roles.

1 CORINTHIANS 6:9 AND 1 TIMOTHY 1:10

> Do you not know that the wicked will not inherit the kingdom of God? Do not be deceived: Neither the sexually immoral nor idolaters nor adulterers nor male prostitutes nor homosexual offenders (1 Cor. 6:9, NIV).

Virtually every Greek lexicon has understood these words (especially *arsenokoitai*) to be referring to homosexuality. Arndt and Gingrich's lexicon says *malakoi* refers to men who are "soft, effeminate, esp[ecially] of catamites, men and boys who allow themselves to be misused homosexually."[1] Likewise, *arsenokoites* means "a male who practices homosexuality, pederast, sodomite."[2]

We also find these terms in classical Greek literature (e.g., Lucian and Aristotle) sometimes applied to obviously gay persons. If Paul were only condemning certain types of homosexuality, he would certainly have specified this. Instead, he used a term directly based on the Greek Septuagint translation of the prohibitions against homosexuality (Lev. 18:22; 20:13). Paul, a rabbi thoroughly trained in the Torah, was certainly mindful of these Levitical condemnations and the Septuagint's translation of them when he chose his wording in 1 Corinthians and 1 Timothy.

In summary, the answer from Scripture is No, Christians are not to be involved in homosexuality nor "approve of those" who are engaged in it (Rom. 1:32, NKJV). I realize it is not "politically correct" to speak critically concerning any person or group's sexual preferences in the twenty-first century. Nonetheless, a true follower of Jesus Christ is committed to modeling the teachings of Scripture. Christ-like love cannot overlook immorality, even when it is politically incorrect to point out the vice. The follower of Christ in the twenty-first century must use Scripture, not culture, as his or her moral compass.

At the same time, we must reach out to all people with the love of Jesus Christ and His gospel, which alone has the power to change lives. And we must speak out against hatred and violence directed toward any group, remembering that we are all sinners, worthy only of God's judgment. Although homosexuality is an easy target in conservative evangelical circles, the truth of the matter is that we all have sin in our lives (Rom. 3:10; 3:23), and we are all tempted in different ways (whether it be toward homosexuality, adultery, lust, incest, greed, violence, pride, gluttony, etc.).

Paul used the law to show us our sin and the fearful judgment awaiting us. Then, to those who truly desire to follow God, he announced the good news of the gospel: "For the wages of sin is death,

---

[1] Walter Bauer, *A Greek-English Lexicon of the New Testament and Other Early Christian Literature*, trans. William F. Arndt and F. Wilbur Gingrich, 2d ed. (Chicago: Univ. of Chicago Press, 1979), p. 488.

[2] *Ibid.*, p. 109.

but the gift of God is eternal life in Jesus Christ our Lord" (Rom. 6:23, NKJV). For all who accept this gift, including homosexuals, there is reconciliation to God. Finally, there is a God-given sisterhood and brotherhood where love can be celebrated without sexual activity and without committing the act of sodomy.

Q: If we have not misinterpreted Scripture, and we condemn homosexuality in the Christian community, then why aren't we also following the rest of the laws set down in the Old Testament? Why are we selective of which parts of the Bible we follow (and point fingers in judgment) and which parts no longer apply to our culture? Is it because when Jesus came, we were set free from the law (Old Testament) by his grace? And now the most important commandments we can keep are to love God with all our heart and love one another? If this is true, then doesn't it apply to everyone as in "Whosoever believes in me..."? Why do some say you cannot be a gay Christian, and you are going to hell if you practice homosexuality? Doesn't that contradict the free gift of God's mercy and grace? If you believe in Jesus and proclaim Him as your Lord and Savior, isn't it okay to live as He created me, in a loving, monogamous relationship? If your life bears good fruit for God's glory, are you not His disciple?

A: It is true that we are no longer obligated to follow the Old Testament civil and ceremonial laws. However, the Old Testament does reveal the moral character of God, thus showing his disapproval of any sexual relationship that is outside of the husband and wife relationship.

Regardless, the New Testament also addresses homosexuality. In Romans 1:18-32 Paul lists homosexuality and lesbianism immediately after idolatry as warning signs that a violation of morality, reason, and nature has occurred (see previous answer).

22

Jesus

Q: Why do Christians believe that Jesus is different from any other religious leader?

First, Jesus fulfilled the documented prophecies describing the Messiah that were recorded centuries before His earthly ministry, including His place of birth (Mic. 5:2; Mt. 2:1-6; Lk. 2:4-11) and type of death (Ex. 12:1-11,46; Ps. 22; Isa. 53:1-7; Zech. 12:10; Mt. 27:31-56; Mk. 15:6-39; Lk. 23:32-46; Jn. 1:29-36; 19:23-36).

Second, Jesus performed numerous miracles, showing that He had complete power and authority over death, nature, sickness, and spiritual forces (Mt. 8:1-4; 12:9-13; Mk. 6:45-52; 10:46-52; Lk. 8:23; 11:14-20; Jn. 2:1-11; 11:38-44).

Third, Jesus claimed to be God and the only way through which men can be saved (Mt. 26:63-64; Jn. 8:58; 11:25-26; 14:6).

Fourth, Jesus rose from the dead on the third day, just as He said He would, and appeared to hundreds of people, even eating and speaking with them (Mt. 12:39-40; Mk. 16:9-13; Lk. 24:6-43; Jn. 2:19-22; 20:1-28; 21:1-14; Acts 1:3-8; 1 Cor. 15:5-8).

Fifth, Jesus transformed the lives of his disciples—men who had witnessed the execution of their leader and went into hiding fearing for their lives were so transformed that they were willing to risk everything to spread the news that Jesus was risen (Mt. 26:69-75; Mk. 14:43-52; 16:9-20; Lk. 24:33-53; Jn. 20:19).

Q: Is there any evidence outside of the Bible that confirms that Jesus was a real person?

A: Yes there is. Josephus, a Jewish historian, and Tacitus, a Roman historian, are two of the most prominent figures that attest that Jesus was a real historical person. In addition to these, there are a number of other ancient manuscripts, both Christian (early creeds and letters of early Church leaders) and non-Christian (Pliny the Younger, Seutonius, Thallus, Emperor Trajan, Emperor Hadrian, and Lucian) that confirm the historicity of Jesus Christ and that His followers believed that He had risen from the dead.

There is also a good collection of lost documents, such as *The Acts of Pontius Pilate*, which other extant ancient manuscripts quoted and referenced, that provide complementary information on the historicity of Jesus.

Q: Isn't it a bit arrogant of Christians to believe that they are right and everyone else (Buddhists, Muslims, etc.) is wrong?

A: Philosophically, the assertion that all religions lead to God is a violation of the Law of Non-Contradiction. Simply put, we cannot all be right because we are all proclaiming different teachings regarding salvation. Jesus Christ made the statement, "I am the way, the truth, and the life. No one comes to the Father except through Me" (Jn. 14:6, NKJV). Therefore, as followers of Christ, we are simply espousing His teachings regarding this issue.

Nevertheless, unlike any other religious leader, Jesus Christ alone has the credentials to back up this claim. He regularly made it clear that He was God, and He possessed the evidence to substantiate His claim with miracles, prophecies, a sinless life, and an empty tomb.

The exclusive nature of salvation is a revelation of truth, and therefore it is not arrogant. Rather, thinking that we can somehow earn or merit salvation through our works and deeds is arrogance. For further study consider reading *The Case for Christ* by Lee Strobel, *More than a Carpenter* by Josh McDowell, and *Postmodernism: What You Should Know and Do About It* by Bobby Brewer (cf. Acts 4:12).

Q: Do I have to hate my family to follow Jesus (cf. Lk. 14:26)?

A: This is a vivid hyperbole from the ancient Near East that simply does not translate very well in twenty-first century English. The meaning of the text explained by Jesus is that one must love Jesus even more than his immediate family. We see an example of this in Matthew 10:37-39, where Jesus demonstrates that mature discipleship entails a commitment to follow Him above anyone else (cf. Mt. 15:1-6).

Q: Where did Jesus go and what did He do during the three days between His death and resurrection?

A: Jesus told the thief on the cross, "Today you will be with me in paradise" (Lk. 23:43, NIV), which often implies a problem because according to Acts 1:9 Jesus did not ascend into heaven until forty days later. Jesus' spirit went immediately to paradise, but His body went to the grave for three days. Jesus said on the cross, "Father, into Your hands I commit My Spirit" (Lk. 23:46, NKJV). Later, when Jesus said to Mary after His resurrection, "I have not yet ascended to My Father" (Jn. 20:17, NKJV), He was referring to His body ascending to heaven forty days after His resurrection, not to His spirit going to heaven between death and resurrection.

Concerning where Jesus was specifically during the three days, His body was in the tomb. The fact that He was resurrected body and soul on the third day confirms His deity and victory over sin and death. Although it is debatable, it is our position that during the three days, Jesus also went to proclaim victory to the "spirits in prison" (1 Pet. 3:19, NKJV; cf. Eph. 4:9). This is sometimes referred to as the "compartmental theory of hades," because it appears that "paradise" was not yet "up in heaven," but in a place where Lazarus was able to see it across the gulf (Lk. 16:22-24).

Following His crucifixion it would appear that Jesus went to proclaim victory to spirit-beings and to relocate "paradise" to heaven. This would seem the most logical conclusion because at the end of 1 Peter 3, Jesus is shown as having authority over all spirit beings (1 Pet. 3:22).

Q: Was Good Friday a designated day of commemoration of Christ's death on the cross by the early Catholic Church? When we try to apply Jesus' words in Matthew 12:40 of three days and three nights in the heart of the earth to Good Friday, it seems they do not match. Is it possible, as others have suggested, that Christ was crucified on Wednesday (before 6:00 P.M. on the Jewish calendar) and was resurrected shortly after Saturday ended (6:00 P.M. on the Jewish calendar—or early Sunday)? Some say that there were two Sabbaths during that week (one high and one regular) so that Mark 15:42 does not conflict. Does this mean that maybe we should look to Wednesday as the day to remember instead of Friday?

A: Initially it does appear slightly confusing because in our western terminology we tend to think of days as complete twenty-four hour periods. However, in the terminology of the ancient Near East a complete twenty-four hour revolution of the earth does not have to take place in order to be reckoned as a day. It was perfectly understandable in their vernacular to count Friday as day one, Saturday as day two, and Sunday as day three. Nevertheless, a number of biblical scholars believe that the crucifixion may have taken place on a Thursday.

23

Judging

Q: *1 Corinthians 5:12-13 seems to suggest that Christians should not judge non-Christians about actions that are wrong. However, does this mean that Christians should never point out wrong when they see it if it is among non-Christians? Wouldn't this be the same as turning a blind-eye towards evil?*

A: The Church is to exercise spiritual discipline over believers (Mt. 18:15-18), but is not authorized to judge the unsaved world. There are governing authorities to do that (Rom. 13:1-5), and the ultimate judgment of the world is to be left to God alone (Rev. 20:11-15). Nevertheless, we are to be "salt to the earth" (Mt. 5:13), and God has also bestowed common sense upon us, and so in some circumstances it is very appropriate to share wisdom and address the sins of others as long as we do so in a loving and non-condescending manner.

In Matthew 7 the Christian is instructed not to judge hypocritically or in a self-righteous manner, but to judge others by the same standard we are judged. The same thought is expressed in Matthew 23:13-39. In Ephesians 5:11 we are told to expose the "deeds of lawlessness" by bringing light to them, but to always speak such truths in love (Eph. 4:14,15).

24

Lying

Q: Is it ethical to lie in some circumstances like Rahab? Is it okay to kill if it is for God as in Gideon killing the Midianites?

A: This is a great question and one with which many theologians and ethicists still struggle. Rahab's act of protecting the spies was a demonstration of faith. She firmly believed that God would destroy Jericho. However, the answer is that although God does reward and affirm Rahab's faith and her desire to honor God, her lying is not affirmed anywhere in Scripture (see Heb. 11:31; Jam. 2:25). Put simply, lying is always a sin. God could have accomplished the rescue without lying.

In regard to Gideon and the destruction of the Midianites, it must be kept in mind that Israel's response was not unprovoked. Judges 6:6 says, "Midian so impoverished the Israelites that they cried out to the Lord for help" (NIV). And God did indeed respond. Archaeologists and ancient Near East studies confirm the ruthlessness of the Midianites and their hostility toward Israel. Although it is somewhat difficult to swallow in today's politically-correct world, the fact is that sometimes God does collectively judge nations. However, He always offers grace should a person or people group choose to repent, as was the case with Rahab and the city of Nineveh described in the book of Jonah.

25

Marriage and Divorce

Q: A Christian co-worker of mine recently found out that her son's girlfriend is pregnant. This young Christian couple was soon to be engaged after dating four years. Because of this situation, my friend does not know if they will be allowed to be married in their church. What's your view?

A: Jesus encountered a similar situation in which He said, "Go and sin no more" (Jn. 8:11, NKJV). Therefore, we would encourage them to abstain from sexual relations until they are married. Here at SBC, we believe that God takes marriage very seriously and that it even serves as a symbol of the relationship between Christ and the Church (Eph. 5:25-27).

Our staff performs weddings for people who are believers and who complete our marriage preparation course. This is because we want to equip our members to have the right tools to be successful in their marriages. We will marry two non-believers, for they are not unequally yoked (2 Cor. 6:14), if they are willing to do the above.

Q: What does the Bible mean when it speaks of adultery? How does it relate to swinging and spouse swapping (assuming that couples are consenting)?

A: By definition, adultery is the act of sexual unfaithfulness by a married man or woman. Biblically, Christ taught that sexual unfaithfulness even includes lust (Mt. 5:28). God created and designed sex to be exclusively between a married man and woman period (see Lk. 19:2-6). Consent by two couples is irrelevant because it does not negate God's view of it as immoral and damaging behavior. Take a good look at 1 Thessalonians 4:1-8.

Q: What does the Bible teach about marriage and remarriage?

A: The Bible clearly teaches that God intended marriage to be permanent (Gen. 2:23-24; Mal. 2:16; Mt. 19:6; Rom. 7:2-3). The Church and Christians are to make every effort to support the permanence of marriage (Mt. 19:1-8). The Bible also recognizes the reality of divorce, and although Scripture never commands or commends divorce, there are circumstances in which it is allowed but regulated. They are:

1.   Adultery/Infidelity. Jesus said, "Whoever divorces his wife, except for immorality, and marries another woman commits adultery" (Mt. 19:9). Even in the case of immorality, strong consideration should be given to forgiveness and the restoration of the marriage relationship whenever possible.

2.   Desertion by an Unsaved Partner. 1 Corinthians 7:15 informs us that a Christian who has been deserted by his or her spouse is no longer bound to the marriage vows.

These are the only two reasons listed in Scripture that permit divorce. God's goal is for reconciliation, and remarriage to anyone other than the original partner is permissible only if the former partner has already remarried (Deut. 24:1-4). Scripture is silent on many issues that affect divorce and remarriage in today¹s society (e.g., spousal abuse), and so we must carefully avoid being legalistic on such issues. Moreover, we certainly do not think these issues should be approached carelessly or flippantly.

Q: How does God view a six-month trial separation? I think God would not think badly of me for choosing a temporary separation over divorce. Staying at this point is breaking my spirit. What do I do? My spouse says he is not in love with me anymore, and he has physically abused me. He hides money and gambles. I have a child with him and have a very unsettling feeling about the security of our future. I have tried communicating my needs and counseling. He claims this is "who he is." How long do I have to tolerate a lonely, empty, sexless marriage with this person? Forever? I cannot imagine God would want that for my life! Help!

A: Thank you for your inquiry and my prayers are with you. Every situation must be evaluated on a case-by-case basis. I would like to recommend that both of you contact our marriage and family department to schedule a counseling appointment. If your spouse is unwilling to attend I would still recommend that you make the appointment.

We know from Scripture that God hates divorce (Mal. 2:16), and that His desire is for your marriage to be permanent. In fact, marriage between a man and woman serves as a daily, visual illustration of His relationship to the Church. At the same time Paul says if the unbeliever leaves, let him leave for we have been called to peace (1 Cor. 7:15). You can rest assured that God in His omniscience knew before you were born that you and your spouse would meet, fall in love, and marry. Likewise, He knew that you would go through a stage in which you questioned your decision, but His desire is to see your marriage continue and thrive. It is most admirable that you have already proactively sought out counseling.

I realize that you must feel exasperated at this point, and generally speaking, based upon the information you have provided, a six-month trial separation may indeed be the right move, but I would not initiate it without first seeking professional Christian counseling. This is a time to draw support from your church family.

Q: My husband and I are having doubts about our marriage. Perhaps God did not want us to get married in the first place. Maybe God had different plans for us. Do you think God would want us to divorce so we can live out His will for us individually? Or will God truly bless our marriage even though we may not have been in His will at the time we married?

A: Thanks for being so candid and transparent. I doubt there is a couple around that has not at one time or another wondered silently or aloud: Did I make a mistake? The problem is that rather than dismissing it as a fleeting thought some couples begin to entertain the idea of divorce. They try to justify their reasoning by emphasizing the problems in their marriage—problems, I might add, that arise in *every* marriage. Regardless, we know from God's Word that it is not His will for you to divorce (Mal. 2:16). Therefore, it is not even an option to consider unless there has been adultery.

I suggest that you and your husband do two things: 1) confess your sin of not yielding to God's will in the past; and 2) promise to make every effort to yield to God's will in the future. Or in the words of Paul,

"[F]orgetting those things which are behind and reaching forward to those things which are ahead, I press toward the goal for the prize of the upward call of God in Christ Jesus" (Php. 3:13b-14, NKJV). This is advice that every Christian, married or single, would do well to heed. God will take your submissive hearts and create something new.

Q: What is Scottsdale Bible Church's position on marriage and divorce?

A: The position of Scottsdale Bible Church (as established by the Board of Elders and Pastoral Staff) is as follows:

God created marriage as a sacred union that reflects the relationship of His Son, Jesus Christ, to His bride, the Church. It is because of the sacredness of this union that God hates divorce (cf. Mal. 2:16). While some may disagree as to whether there are biblical grounds for divorce, there is agreement that no more than two may exist: adultery and desertion (Mt. 19:9; 1 Cor. 7:15). Divorce is never commanded nor is it ever God's perfect will for a person's life.

THE PASTORAL POSITION (AS AGREED UPON BY THE PASTORS):

REGARDING DIVORCE:

We never counsel a Christian to seek a divorce for any reason (cf. Mt. 5:31-32,19:1-12; Mk. 10:2-12; Lk. 16:18).

REGARDING REMARRIAGE:

- If the mate is deceased, the husband or wife is free to remarry (cf. Rom. 7:2; 1 Cor. 7:39).
- A person divorced before becoming a Christian has the following clear alternatives: to remarry former spouse (if not remarried) or to remain unmarried. Since our understanding of Scripture is uncertain as to the freedom to marry another, we leave this decision to the individual and the Pastor to carry out their own conviction based upon their study of Scripture (cf. 1 Cor. 7:8-15).
- A Christian divorced by a Christian without biblical grounds has the following clear alternatives: to remarry their former spouse (if not remarried) or to remain unmarried (cf. 1 Cor. 7:10-11).
- A Christian divorced by an adulterous mate has the freedom

to remain unmarried. Since our understanding of Scripture is uncertain as to the freedom to marry another, we leave this decision to the individual and the Pastor to carry out their own conviction based upon their study of Scripture (cf. Mt. 19:9).

- A Christian abandoned and divorced by an unbeliever has the following clear alternatives: to be remarried to their former spouse (if not remarried) or to remain unmarried. Since our understanding of Scripture is uncertain as to the freedom to marry another, we leave this decision to the individual and the Pastor to carry out their own conviction based upon their study of Scripture (cf. 1 Cor. 7:12-15).

OUR POSITION ON ELDER AND PASTORAL LEADERSHIP OF SCOTTSDALE BIBLE CHURCH:

An Elder is to be "above reproach" (1 Tim. 3:2). He also must be "the husband of one wife" (1 Tim. 3:2, NKJV). The question is whether this passage disqualifies a man with a divorce in his past. Our understanding of this qualification is that it speaks of a man's devotion to his own wife. This passage should not be used to automatically disqualify a man from service if there has been a divorce in the past. Questions must be asked as to the circumstances of the divorce. Was it before becoming a believer? Were there biblical grounds? How long ago was it? To disqualify a man when the Scriptures do not flirts with legalism, going beyond the Scriptures.

Q: I have always struggled with what I perceive the Church's position is on divorce, especially when it comes to women who are abused and who live in constant fear. Is it God's will that these women remain married? Is it fair that if these women are able to get divorced that they cannot commit themselves to a partner ever again? Can you tell me how a woman in this situation is forgiven and possibly able to move forward with her life?

A: The Bible clearly teaches that God intended marriage to be permanent (Gen. 2:23-24), and thus Christians and the Church are to make every effort to support and communicate the permanence of marriage. At SBC, our understanding of divorce and remarriage is based on the Bible. We want to relate meaningfully to our society and the problems people face. We are well aware that marriage is a two-vote system. Both parties must vote "Yes" in its favor and for its permanence. If just one person votes "No," regardless of the other person's commitment and desire for the marriage to remain intact, the relationship typically dissolves.

Biblically, divorce is never commanded or commended. God's desire is for reconciliation. However, there are two cases addressed in the Bible in which divorce is allowed: (1) Adultery (Infidelity) is a condition that permits divorce. Jesus said, "Whoever divorces his wife, except for immorality, and marries another woman commits adultery" (Mt. 19:9). (2) Desertion is the other biblical basis for divorce (1 Cor. 7:15). In such a case, the Christian who has been deserted is "no longer under bondage" (i.e. to the marriage vows). However, the implication here is that an unbelieving spouse left because of their partner's conversion.

What About Remarriage?

Biblically, if divorce is for the reasons above, remarriage is permitted, but if it is for any other reason besides the above, the only remarriage that is permitted is to the original partner (1 Cor. 7:10-11). However, if the original partner has remarried, there is no longer an opportunity for reconciliation and thus the deserted or innocent party *may* (see above) be free to remarry (Deut. 24:1-4).

Q: Is physical abuse biblical grounds to divorce?

A: The Bible does not address this specific issue but we certainly do not think God would expect you to remain in an abusive relationship in which your health, and possibly even your life, would be jeopardized. Romans 13:1-7 tells us that God has provided the government as a minister for the innocent. Our government, in this case, does provide for legal restraints and legal separation.

26

Money and Finances

Q: Is it a sin to file bankruptcy due to one's failure in handling his or her monies?

A: If your primary problem is overspending on consumables, such as food, gas, clothing, and vacations, these have to be brought under control or no plan will succeed, not even bankruptcy. You must develop a budget that is as non-indulgent as possible. Once you know exactly what you need to live on, determine how much money is left over to pay creditors. Divide it proportionally among your creditors, and write each of them a letter asking them to work with you. Include a copy of your budget and a chart of creditors. Explain that you're unable to pay what you promised, but you will pay according to your budget. As you have any additional income from the sale of your home, cars, boat, motor home, or other assets; from tax refunds or gifts; from a part-time job, overtime pay, salary increases, or bonuses use this to help retire your debts. You also could pay off debt with retirement funds, if you have any.

Most creditors would far rather have something than nothing. The only reason that most creditors get angry or nasty is because people avoid them, rather than being honest. A word of caution is necessary here. Any time there has been overspending and there does not seem to be enough income, it will take six to nine months before your budget balances on a month-to-month basis. Obviously, you did not get into debt in three months, and you are not going to get out in three months. It will take several months to develop the routine of living within your budget. Your resolve will be tested by everything from car repairs to washing machine breakdowns.

Do not quit simply because the budget does not work in the first few months. Stay with it and do not get discouraged. It is a lot of fun to get into debt; it is not nearly as much fun to get out. It requires discipline, but once you commit yourself to doing what is right, do not look back. Stick it out. If you have totally surrendered your finances to God and you're willing to obey his principles, God will be faithful and just to forgive you, and to provide what you need on a month-to-month basis. He promises to meet your needs, and you can claim that promise. But first, you have to stop overspending and trust Him.

If you would like more information on Biblical Stewardship, please attend our "Coinonia" class on Sunday mornings. It exists to help people understand what God's Word says about finances and to help them develop a monthly spending plan.

27

Movies and Media

Q: In our groups on Wednesday night we discussed the influence of television shows, music, movies, etc. Where do I draw the line when it comes to filtering out the bad? If I do not know what is going on in the culture that I live in can I really help?

A: This question is difficult to provide a general answer to and it requires that you be true and honest to yourself. If you notice that a particular program is having a negative influence on your (or a fellow believer's) spiritual growth then it is important that you acknowledge it and refrain from putting yourself (or a fellow believer) into a situation that will invite temptation or inhibit spiritual growth (read Rom. 4).

It is important for us to know and understand our culture while not allowing it to alter our Christian worldview. I like to use the analogy of a ship. It is designed to travel on and through water, and yet if it takes on too much water it will sink. Jesus said,

> My prayer is not that you take them out of the world but that you protect them from the evil one. They are not of the world, even as I am not of it. Sanctify them by the truth; your word is truth. As you sent me into the world, I have sent them into the world. For them I sanctify myself, that they too may be truly sanctified (Jn. 17:15-19).

Q: What is your take on Harry Potter's popularity? Do you think it is nothing more than a child's fairy tale? On the other hand, do you think it is a hidden or blatant attempt to propagate Wicca or witchcraft?

A: This is an area where we have to use discernment and one where we must be careful that we do not cause a weaker brother of sister to stumble. I, for example, would consider taking a child over the age of eleven to it and then discussing it afterwards. However, I feel that children eleven and younger may be too impressionable, and I would rather that they not be impressed with the occult, especially if they are not born again.

Unlike most science fiction and fantasy story lines, the problem here is that witchcraft is indeed a real medium into the world of spiritual darkness. The Bible, of course, clearly condemns witchcraft as a practice that is not neutral but evil (Deut. 18:10; Gal. 5:20; Rev. 21:8). I think the most disbelieved verse in the Bible is probably Ephesians 6:12,

> For our struggle is not against flesh and blood, but against the rulers, against the powers, against the world forces of this darkness, against the spiritual forces of wickedness in the heavenly places.

I have seen several interviews with the author and she does not claim to be a witch or to have any ties with the occult. When we bring light to our children we expose darkness. Teach your children the wisdom of discernment.

28

Prayer

Q: *What do you think of the book* The Prayer of Jabez?

A: I am thrilled, of course, that more people are excited and interested in prayer. However, I personally try to model the prayer of Jesus rather than the prayer of Jabez, because it provides us with a more complete picture of prayer. In Luke 11:1 the disciples requested, "Lord, teach us to pray," and Christ then provided a model for them. As a result, our prayer life is to bring us into closer fellowship with God by adoring Him, worshipping Him, praising Him, thanking Him, and then making our supplications known to Him through prayer.

Q: *Our country is diverse in race and religions. After the terrible tragedy on September 11, 2001, many religious groups came together to unite and pray. Should Christians attend multi-faith prayer meetings? If so, what is our response when we are called upon to stand or bow our heads as the participants pray to other gods? I would never want to grieve the Lord or give the impression of having other gods before him.*

A: We are clearly to never bow and worship anyone other than God (Ex. 20:3-5). Only He is worthy of our worship. Over the years I have been at several multi-faith gatherings. I think it is okay to attend such events because it presents us with an opportunity to build friendships with nonbelievers. However, at such events I have never been compelled to worship someone other than God and politely and quietly abstain from any action that would grieve the Holy Spirit. Although others around me may indeed be worshipping someone other than God, I can be in such a gathering and praise the one true God.

Q: The people that I am dealing with have already made up their minds and have turned their backs on God. I pray for these people on a regular basis, but unlike all my other prayers, I do not seem to be receiving an answer either way. Is there anything else I can do? I am brokenhearted over these people because they are very important to me. In fact, one of them is my mother.

A: My heart goes out to you and I can relate to the dilemma of not being able to get through. However, let me encourage you to continue praying for them. I firmly believe that the least believed verse in the Bible is Ephesians 6:12, "We wrestle not against flesh and blood but against...the rulers of the darkness of this age." We are called to communicate the good news, and from there we must trust the Holy Spirit to convict and convince them of God's love and desire to fellowship with them.

Therefore, let me encourage you to continue praying for them. It has been my experience that personal evangelism is often a process. Rarely do I get to be the one to take a person from beginning to end. Rather, I have noticed that sometimes I am simply somewhere in the chain in communicating the gospel to them (1 Cor. 3:6-9). So perhaps God will utilize other believers within their circles to get through in areas in which you cannot.

If they are open to reading I would recommend a book such as *The Case for Christ* by Lee Strobel or *More Than a Carpenter* by Josh McDowell. If they live in the area invite them to attend a worship service with you. You may also want to consider taking the *Becoming a Contagious Christian* course in personal evangelism that we offer twice a year here at SBC.

Q: In this time of national tragedy (September 11, 2001) can you please provide guidance as for whom I should pray? I am confused if I should pray for those responsible. I have a strong conflict within my family and in my own heart about the truly evil acts and the people who facilitate them. It's a no-brainer to pray for those affected, for our leaders, for rescue workers, for the innocents these evil people hide behind, and for the spirit of our country as a whole. But what about our enemies themselves? It's hard for me to understand.

A: It is indeed a hard time to pray. There were several times immediately following the crisis in which I found myself speechless before the Lord.

We are blessed to have the Holy Spirit groan for us at these times (Rom. 8:26). I have been praying for:

- God to protect our nation and to thwart the plans of the wicked.
- Comfort to those who have lost loved ones.
- Strength and protection for the rescue workers, paramedics, firemen, and police workers.
- A spiritual awakening in our nation in which people will realize the existence and implications of evil, the brevity of life, and their need for Jesus.
- The Lord to return quickly. Only then will we have certain and sustained peace.

29

Religions

Q: What is the major difference between Mormonism and Christianity? I know Mormonism is referred to as a cult and I would like to know why. Some of my friends are Mormon and I would like to know how you handle them.

A: The one major difference that stands out between Christianity and religion is Do vs. Done.[1] Religion is about DO—doing works, deeds, etc., in the hope of meriting everlasting life and favor with God. With Jesus it is DONE. He paid the price for humanity's sins, and therefore it is by grace that we are saved by placing our faith in Him for our forgiveness (Jn. 3:16; Eph. 2:8,9).

Q: Recently a friend of mine floored me with the news that she visited a psychic and is exploring the area of New Age spiritual enlightenment. She is looking into the areas of past lives and reading books on these subjects. Can you help me with biblical facts and the roots of this area?

A: A number of issues should concern your friend regarding New Age spirituality. Most New Age leaders are proponents of a belief that we are all deity, whereas Scripture maintains that only the triune God is classified as deity. The teaching that we could be "gods" was first seen in Genesis 3:5, where Satan tempted Eve with the possibility of "being like God." Therefore, not to sound sarcastic, this movement would more accurately be termed as "Old Age" because its false doctrine has been around since Eden.

---

[1]Bill Hybels, *Becoming A Contagious Christian* (Grand Rapids: Zondervan, 1995).

Only God is god. In spite of their claims to be deity, New Agers cannot control the weather; heal leprosy; create food to feed five thousand; restore life to the deceased; live a perfect, sinless life, and rise again. Only Jesus Christ has the credentials to back up His claim of deity. New Agers cannot.

New Age doctrine contradicts God's revelation of truth in the Bible:

REINCARNATION

Hebrews 9:27 tells us that "it is appointed unto man once to die, but after this the judgment" (KJV). Thus, according to God's revelation there is no past life, and as implied by the latter half of the verse, either an eternity with or without God, but not another earthly life.

SALVATION

Most New Age proponents and authors deny the exclusivity of salvation through Jesus Christ. Jesus made it very clear in John 14:6 that He is the way, the truth, and the life and that no one comes to the Father except through Him.

Therefore, we cannot accept New Age teachings as they were meant to be understood because they stand in contradiction to the Bible and essential Christian doctrine.

Q: My husband and I have been blessed with Christian friends whose company we enjoy. We have spent considerable time with them exchanging ideas— talking about work, religion, and the Bible. We have even attended SBC together. Our friends seem to have it all together. They credit a personal coach who helps them meditate and seek their higher self to gain wisdom and answers to concerns. My questions are: How does this New Age practice fit into Christian philosophy? Are we able to "create" our own circumstances and outcomes? Is the correct approach to life "God willing," or "take control," or somewhere in the middle?

A: Put simply, New Age practices do not and should not coincide with Christianity. It is typical of our postmodern culture in which Americans approach spirituality like Luby's cafeteria: "a little Jesus please, and yes, I'll have some Eastern meditation. I'll pass on the palm readings and horoscopes today, but yes I would like a scoop of reincarnation." There is no doubt that the mind is an incredibly powerful organ, and yet it is well documented that it can easily be manipulated. James

Mesmer, from whom we get the word "mesmerize," was one of the first hypnotists to demonstrate and document this phenomenon.

There are numerous references to meditation in the Bible, especially in the Psalms. However, the focus of the mediation is upon God, His attributes, and His revealed Word. Furthermore, Jesus Christ is our mediator (1 Tim. 2:5) and the Holy Spirit is our helper (Jn. 14:16,17), and thus born-again believers do not need a coach.

I know it "appears" that they have it all together, but I would like to encourage you to continue to walk worthy and be a witness to your friends. Only Jesus can truly fulfill their spiritual hunger. Keep encouraging your friends to attend SBC and maybe you could even invite them to attend Class 100 together.

Q: How would you describe the difference between being spiritual and being religious?

A: Being spiritual, in Christian terms, implies that a person is striving to be under the influence of the Holy Spirit and thus in fellowship with God. Being religious means that a person may practice certain rituals but is not necessarily indwelt by the Holy Spirit. The biggest difference is do vs. done (Eph. 2:8-10). Religion is about doing certain acts to gain merit. With Jesus Christ it is done (2 Cor. 5:21). He lived the perfect life for us (the kind of life we could not live) and sent the Comforter, the Holy Spirit, to minister to those who are born again (Jn. 14:16,17). The life we live is a life that pleases God (Gal. 2:20).

30

Salvation

Q: What does Scripture say regarding the salvation of a child who dies before reaching the age of accountability (i.e., when the child has the mental capacity to be aware of the implications and ramifications of being a follower of Jesus Christ)?

A: When the child that David and Bathsheba conceived out of wedlock died, David said in 2 Samuel 12:23b, "I shall go to him, but he shall not return to me" (NKJV), implying that the child was in the presence of God. Therefore, we can deduce that in these situations, such as when a child is unable to mentally understand sin or their need for forgiveness, that Jesus graciously applies His sacrifice to them as their High Priest (Heb. 10:10) and receives them into heaven (cf. Mt. 18:1-6).

Q: Is it possible to accept Christ after you die?

A: Hebrews 9:27 tells us that it is appointed unto man once to die and *after* this the judgment. Jesus' account of the Rich Man and Lazarus in Luke 16 further illustrates and supports this premise. We can therefore conclude that after death it would be too late to convert.

Q: Is there salvation for people of other faiths who are never exposed to Jesus Christ? Or are they simply damned to hell?

A: First, we know from the Bible that it is not God's will that any should perish (Jn. 3:16; 2 Pet. 3:9). Likewise, Acts 4:12 makes it very clear that "Salvation is found in no one else, for there is no other name under heaven given to men by which we must be saved" (NIV). Jesus can apply His sacrifice to whomever He chooses (Heb. 10:10), but He has called us to share the gospel.

Philosophically, the assertion that other and/or many ways lead to God is a violation of the Law of Non-Contradiction. Simply put, we cannot all be right because we are all proclaiming different teachings on salvation. Islam believes in salvation through works and that each man receives his own harem upon entering paradise. Buddhism believes in reincarnation. Hinduism believes that everything, including the book you are now reading, is God.

Jesus Christ made the statement, "I am the way, the truth, and the life. No one comes to the Father except through Me" (Jn. 14:6, NKJV). Therefore, as followers of Christ, we are simply espousing His teachings regarding this issue. Nevertheless, unlike any other religious leader, Jesus Christ alone has the credentials to back up this claim because He was God. He regularly made it clear that He was God and possessed the evidence to substantiate His claim with miracles, prophecies, a sinless life, and an empty tomb.

Therefore, the exclusive nature of salvation is a revelation of truth, and Jesus commissioned us to carry the Good News to the uttermost parts of earth (Acts 1:8). In Romans Paul said, "How, then, can they call on the one they have not believed in? And how can they believe in the one of whom they have not heard?" (Rom. 10:14a). Personal evangelism should be as natural to the Christian as prayer, worship, Bible reading, etc., but somehow it has become an elective in the lives of many North American Christians.

In addition to reaching our own communities we should also spread the Good News to the uttermost parts of the earth by praying for our missionaries who are in largely non-evangelized areas, supporting them financially, going on short-term trips, and/or by prayerfully considering becoming a missionary to one of these people groups. For further study consider reading *The Case for Faith* by Lee Strobel.

Q: Do we as Christians believe once saved, always saved, or can you lose this gift?

A: We believe that if a person was genuinely reborn they cannot lose their salvation. John 3:16 tells us that "whosoever believes in him shall not perish but have everlasting life" (NKJV). Everlasting means to have a beginning but no end. Also, let me encourage you to read Philippians

1:6; Romans 8:28-39; 1 John 2:19; John 10:27-30; and Ephesians 1:13,14; 4:30.

Q: Can a person who accepted Christ later renounce their faith and have their heart so hardened that they lose their salvation?

A: The ultimate question is whether they were born again in the first place. Theologically, it is impossible for a person to lose their salvation if they were truly born again in the first place because once a person has placed their faith in Christ for their salvation they are justified and are adopted into the family of God (see 1 Jn. 2:19; Rom. 8:15-39).

Q: When is a person's name recorded in the Lamb's Book of Life? Is everyone's name recorded at birth and then blotted out if they do not accept Christ as Savior?

A: The Bible does not tell us specifically when our names are recorded in the Lamb's Book of Life (Rev. 20:15), and therefore we are left to speculation. It is also noteworthy that some evangelical Bible scholars interpret the Book of Life metaphorically rather than literally. Regardless, what we know for certain is that God *knows* those who have placed their faith in Him and their eternity is secure in Him. In fact, Revelation 3:5 says, "He who overcomes [born again]...I will never blot out his name from the book of life, but will acknowledge his name before my Father and his angels" (NIV).

Q: My question deals with eternity and heaven. Can a non-Christian (i.e. Jewish, Muslim, Buddhist) enter into God's kingdom of heaven? In other words, can we as Christians expect to experience eternity with our brothers and sisters of other faiths?

A: Salvation is only available through Jesus. It was Jesus who said, "I am the way, the truth, and the life" (Jn. 14:6). Acts 4:12 says, "There is salvation in no one else; for there is no other name under heaven that has been given among men, by which we must be saved." Therefore, as followers of Christ, we are simply espousing His teachings regarding this issue. Nevertheless, unlike any other religious leader, Jesus Christ alone has the credentials to back up His claims of deity and the ability to forgive sin. He regularly made it clear that He was God and possessed the evidence to substantiate His claim with miracles, prophecies, a sinless life, and an empty tomb. No other religious leader possesses these credentials.

Secondly, from a philosophical viewpoint, to teach that all religions lead to God would be a violation of the Law of Non-Contradiction. We simply cannot all be right because we are all teaching different and contradictory doctrines of salvation.

Perhaps the biggest difference between Christianity and Religion is "Do vs. Done." Religion is about what a person has to "do" through works, deeds, etc., in order to merit salvation. Whereas with Jesus it is "Done," in that He lived the perfect life for us and died in our place as a sacrifice for our sins. He, being God, is the only one who can offer forgiveness and everlasting life. Religion, religious leaders, and great humanitarians do not have the credentials to forgive sin and offer everlasting life because they are not God. However, God's invitation is open to all regardless of their cultural or religious background (Rom. 10:9-10; Rev. 3:20).

Q: My mother is a Mormon and rejects the divinity of Jesus. Is it possible for her to "accept Jesus as her Savior" even though she denies His divinity?

A: A person does not need to be a theologian or have a vast understanding of Christian theology in order to accept Christ as Savior. However, in this case, it is important that a person believe in the deity of Jesus Christ because that very credential enables Him to be the only eligible candidate to offer salvation and forgiveness (Jn. 1:1; 3:16; 14:6; Rom. 3:10). John tells us he wrote his gospel so that we might believe Jesus is the Christ, the Son of God, and by believing that we might be saved (Jn. 20:31).

Q: How was it that people in Old Testament times were saved without really having the knowledge of Jesus Christ? Obviously this was prior to His death on the cross and His resurrection. Did salvation come from following God's Law? I know Scripture clearly teaches that man simply cannot follow the Law in a perfect manner. In addition, God always looks at the heart. What did it take for someone to be saved prior to the death and resurrection of Christ?

A: Salvation has always been through faith. The Old Testament Law was never meant to be a means of salvation. Paul tells us in Romans 4 that Abraham and David were justified by faith. Just as we now look back two thousand years to the cross, the Old Testament believers looked forward to it. In fact, most of the ceremonial laws were symbolic of the redemption that Christ would bring. The death, burial, and resurrection of Jesus Christ was the unfolding and realization of the promises and grace anticipated and foretold in the Old Testament.

Christ was the focus and aim of the Mosaic Law (Rom. 10:14). As early as Genesis 15:6 it was revealed that "Abram believed God and he was credited with righteousness." This is very insightful because it was centuries later that God introduced the Mosaic Law. Likewise, the first circumcision did not occur until after this event (Gen. 17). Thus, all the saints in the Old Testament believed in the Messiah who was to come just as we believe He already has. Had this not been the case in the Old Testament era, the writer of Hebrews could not have claimed that the same gospel that had been preached to us was the gospel that had also been preached in the wilderness (Heb. 4:2).

Q: Is one who has never repented truly born again? Or can one be saved without repentance?

A: This is a great question and one that has brought about a number of volumes of books on the topic, especially in the late 1980s. Of course, the answer to the question as to whether or not an individual is genuinely saved is one that only the Lord and the individual in question can know. We risk placing ourselves in a precarious position when trying to measure salvation status by one's outward works. However, I can most certainly relate to the question.

The danger is in the interpretation of "repent," because if we insist on various actions to be performed prior to salvation then we have fallen into the category of being a works-based religion which would be the opposite of what is taught in Ephesians 2:8-9. Paul also vehemently warned against adding to the gospel (Gal 1:6-10). The thief on the cross, for example, did not have the opportunity to perform any acts.

There is nothing a lost, degenerate, spiritually-dead sinner can do that will contribute to salvation. Repentance, commitment, and obedience are all divine works, wrought by the Holy Spirit in the heart of everyone who is saved. If a person is born again and not walking worthy, they become subject to God's chastisement (Heb. 12:5-8). Salvation establishes the root that will produce the fruit of the Spirit and good works (Eph. 2:10).

However, a mere acknowledgment of the facts of the gospel (and/or the historicity of Jesus) alone is not enough to save. Salvation is more than just mere lip service to the biblical facts regarding the death, burial, and resurrection of Jesus Christ. Paul addresses "faith-plus-anything theology" in his correction of the believers in Galatia about the error of adding circumcision to faith. Salvation is conditioned solely on faith in Jesus Christ. That faith must be placed in Christ as one's substitute for and Savior from sin. This naturally implies that a person is cognizant of the fact that they are a sinner, they desire forgiveness (thus implying some degree of remorse), and they are in need of redemption.

Some of the confusion seems to involve the aspect of sanctification. Submitting to the Lordship of Christ is a part of sanctification and discipleship, but it cannot begin until a person has actually been born again. It is a result of salvation, which is an instantaneous act of God. It is not earned and does not demand a repayment. To demand such would be paying a wage and requiring a service.

In summary, the more biblical position is actually in the middle of the two views (lordship salvation and faith alone) and that the two have more in common than they realize. Although this may sound like a safe and non-committal answer, what is meant is that although a non-believer should be willing to repent, it is not a prerequisite that he or she should first "get their life right" before they are eligible for salvation. Nor should any pre-salvific work be attached to the message of grace. This is based on the fact that for a person to ask for forgiveness is itself an acknowledgement of their status as a sinner and thus remorse at their circumstance. There should be grave concern with the Lordship position in cases where it tends to promote pre-salvific works, because such a theology places itself in the dangerous position of adding conditions to the gospel message other than faith and trust for salvation in the work of Christ. And there should be a grave concern with cheapening the gospel of the One called the Lord Jesus Christ.

31

Theology

Q: Who were some of the great teachers or theologians throughout the years?

A: The development and study of Christian history and theology is a fascinating and worthwhile study. Paul, of course, would be the first and most prominent theologian and church leader following Jesus Christ. James was the first pastor of the church in Jerusalem following Pentecost.

There were a number of significant church fathers following the death of the apostles such as Tertullian and Polycarp, but we must remember that Scripture is the final arbitrator of Christian doctrine. Generally, as is the case today, you will find that you will largely agree with post-apostolic theologians, but from time to time you find a few tenets of their teachings that may conflict with orthodox Christian doctrine.

Nevertheless, to answer your question, most historians recognize Augustine (354-430) as the most notable of the early theologians following the apostles. He is also one of the few theologians who could also be considered a philosopher. Likewise, secular and Christian historians concur that Thomas Aquinas (1225-74) is another major contributor to the articulation and development of Christian theology.

Other major contributors would include John Wycliffe (1320-1384), John Calvin (1509-64), Zwingli (1484-1531), and Martin Luther (1483-1546). Some would consider C.S. Lewis and Francis Schaeffer to have been the most recent contributors to Christian thought, and a *Time* magazine article once proclaimed Schaeffer as "the brightest Christian mind of the 20th century."

If you have an interest in Christian theology and philosophy, I would encourage you to consider familiarizing yourself with their writings. One of the better books on the subject is *The Story of Christian Theology* by Roger E. Olson.

Q: I am taking an American Literature class at ASU and reading a lot about the Puritans who embraced Calvinism. Although SBC teaches some tenets of Calvinism, it doesn't seem like it totally conforms to it. How does SBC respond to Calvinism? Do you teach predestination? What is all the debate about between Calvinists and non-Calvinists?

A: At SBC we thank God for John Calvin's contributions in articulating Christian doctrine and theology. However, you are correct in that although we do reflect the vast majority of Calvinism's tenets, as a rule we do not consider ourselves to be a "Calvinistic"[1] or "non-Calvinistic" church per se, but simply a Bible church. I realize that at first glance this may sound like a rather non-committal answer but I believe that we should heed Paul's counsel in his letter to the church at Corinth in which he said,

> For I have been informed concerning you, my brethren...that there are quarrels among you...that each of you is saying, "I am of Paul," and "I of Apollos," and "I of Cephas," and "I of Christ." Has Christ been divided? Paul was not crucified for you, was he? Or were you baptized in the name of Paul? (1 Cor. 1:11-13).

My point is that it would be just as applicable to insert any great Christian leader's name in place of Apollos, etc., but we must remember that God's Word is the final arbitrator of truth.

The area of Calvinism that seems to cause the most debate and confusion has to do with the Calvinistic (also known as Reformed Theology) doctrines of double predestination and limited atonement.[2]

---

[1] It is noteworthy that not all of what falls under the umbrella of Calvinism necessarily reflects the beliefs and teachings of John Calvin. Likewise, as in nearly all systems, there is not universal agreement among Calvinists on Calvinistic doctrine.

[2] Predestination generally is a reference to the belief that before creation, God chose who would go to heaven. Limited atonement is generally a reference to the belief that Jesus only died for these elect.

It has been my personal experience that much of the confusion is actually over semantics. Nearly all evangelicals believe that God is absolutely and completely sovereign over all creation and its history. Paul makes it clear God ultimately chooses who will respond to Him (Eph. 1:4), but to add that He must also choose those who are lost is to use human logic without a clear statement to this effect from Scripture.

Likewise, nearly all evangelicals believe that God loves all sinners and that Jesus died for all of humanity, but technically speaking only believers benefit from His offer of forgiveness and atonement. As Dr. Wayne Grudem says, "[t]o say that Jesus came to offer eternal life to the world is not to say that he actually paid the penalty for the sins of everyone who would ever live."[3] It is quite clear that not everyone experiences the new birth (Rev. 20:15; cf. Hell). "Likewise, when Paul says that Christ 'gave himself as a ransom *for all* '(1 Tim. 2:6), we are to understand this to mean a ransom *available* (italics mine) for all people, without exception."[4] This does *not* mean that all of humanity is saved.

As to double predestination, we believe it may logically follow that if God chose those who will respond to Him (Eph. 1:4), He must have also chosen who would not. Because this is not clearly stated and rests on human logic, we do not teach this understanding.

In summary, let me say that, depending on who you talk to, not all Calvinists would concur with the way we have represented their beliefs as defined above. I also believe that we should be careful not to think more highly of ourselves than we ought by presuming that our three pound brains can completely comprehend the mind of God regarding His omniscience and sovereignty and mankind's ability to freely choose. While these subjects provide stimulating intellectual conversation we do not feel that they are issues to divide over.

Q: Does SBC align itself with the five points of Calvinism? If not, how does it differ?

A: At SBC we try to avoid labeling ourselves due to the fact that there are various interpretations associated with each label which may or

---

[3]Wayne Grudem, *Systematic Theology* (Grand Rapids: Zondervan, 1994), p. 588.

[4]*Ibid*, p. 589.

may not accurately reflect our (or their) views. However, to answer your question, at SBC we would lean towards a dispensational view, yet we also strongly agree with the vast majority of what's known as Reformation Theology and/or Calvinism, and therefore you could also consider us to be "moderate Calvinists." However, the points we would differ on are not essential Christian doctrine. Therefore it can provide stimulating intellectual discussion but should not cause division within the body of Christ.

The five points are TULIP: Total Depravity of Mankind, Unconditional Election, Limited Atonement, Irresistible Grace, and Perseverance of the Saints.

First, we do agree with all of the points with the exception of Limited Atonement, but we should clarify that we believe in perseverance of the saints only to the degree of eternal security. We do not believe there is scriptural support to indicate that a believer will perpetually live a godly and Christ-like life and/or will repent prior to death.

We acknowledge God's omniscience and sovereignty yet we disagree with some of our Calvinist friends who teach double predestination (supralapsarianism), which teaches that before the Fall God had already decreed who would go to heaven and who would go to hell. Thus, how could the reprobate be held accountable for their sins if God has already decreed their eternal destiny? It would also seem to make God the author of evil, which would be a violation of His immutability and holiness.

This belief (supralapsarianism) is also linked with the view of Limited Atonement, which teaches that Jesus only died for the elect. We know from the Bible that Jesus died for all of humanity (Jn. 3:16; 1 Jn. 2:2), and that it is not His will that any should perish (2 Pet. 3:9). Likewise, we have been commissioned to spread the Good News (Mt. 28:19,20). The atonement was enough for all, yet only the elect will receive its application.

We believe this is a part of the mystery of God in that both God's omniscience and humanity's free will are evident in the Bible. We believe in election (Eph. 1:4), and yet in God's infinite wisdom man's choices effect his eternal destiny (Josh. 24:15; Rom. 10:13). We will meet with our Five-Point Calvinist sisters and brothers in heaven and then know for certain how God's sovereignty and mankind's free will actually fit together in the mind of God. We believe it is unwise to limit infinite wisdom to our finite understanding.

Q: I am confused by the following terms: dispensationalism, reformed theology, and covenant theology. Can you shed some light on these terms?

A: There are various schools of thought within each of these theological schemes, but generally speaking we can define them as follows:

Dispensationalism as articulated by J.N. Darby in the nineteenth century believes in a distinction between Israel and the Church as two groups in God's overall plan for humanity and that there are seven different historical periods or *dispensations* (e.g., Pre-Fall Age of Innocence, Noahic covenant through Sinatic covenant, etc.) in how God related and revealed Himself to His creation. (There are some proponents of the dispensational school who believe that there were different modes of salvation in each of these periods). However, most dispensationalists teach that all of the previous eras pointed to Christ and that salvation has always been through faith in God (Gen. 15:6).

Reformed theology is a much broader term. Technically, it refers to a systematic theology that reflects the principles of the Protestant Reformation (1517). In a narrower sense, it is heavily influenced by the theology and teachings of John Calvin, John Knox, and Ulrich Zwingli. In fact, some people refer to it as "Calvinistic theology." The three predominant principles of Reformed Theology would be salvation by grace alone, the ultimate authority of Scripture, and the priesthood of all believers. Reformed theologians later developed a doctrine that is described by the acronym "TULIP":

Total Depravity—humans are dead in trespasses and sins before God sovereignly regenerates them and gives them the gift of salvation.

Unconditional election—God chooses some humans to save before and apart from anything they do on their own.

Limited Atonement—Christ died only to save the elect, and his atoning death is not universal for all of humanity.

Irresistible Grace—God's grace cannot be resisted. The elect will receive it and be saved by it. The damned never will.

Perseverance—The elect will inevitably persevere unto final salvation (eternal security).[5]

Covenant theologians generally believe that the eschatological promises made to Abraham (Israel) are still intact, but that there is a new covenant which is now available through Jesus Christ, in which we now have the potential to be one body, Jew and Gentile alike, and no longer need to adhere to the civil and ceremonials laws as described in the Old Testament. This is not to be confused with "Two Covenant" theology, which incorrectly teaches that salvation for the Jews is still available by adhering to the Old Testament law, and salvation for the Gentiles is available through Jesus. The Church is the New Israel and all promises to Israel are fulfilled in the Church.

Q: Why does an all-powerful and holy God allow evil and suffering to exist?

A: If God had wanted to He could have created a race of mindless robots that would always obey Him. However, it appears that God wants people to love and worship Him because they want to do so. In many respects this is the theme of the book of Job. This freedom of choice (that even the angels apparently had) necessitates that mankind have the ability to choose wrong. In fact, most of the sin and evil in the world is the result of humans sinning against other humans. God is not aloof to the effects of sin and evil. He experienced it firsthand (e.g., at the cross). Due to His sacrifice for the sins of all humanity, He has done something about it in that He offers forgiveness and an afterlife in heaven. He will also return one day to "set things straight" per se.

Q: If God already knows who will accept Him as Savior and who will reject Him why should we even bother to evangelize?

A: Because God has commanded us to do so (Mt. 28:19,20). Actually, this should give us even more confidence and boldness for personal evangelism because we know that there are others out there who are

---

[5]Roger Olson, *The Story of Christian Theology* (Downers Grove, IL: InterVarsity Press, 1999, p. 460.

not yet a part of God's Kingdom. In other words, there are still many pre-Christians that we interact with who will indeed respond positively to the gospel message.

Paul said, "I endure everything for the sake of the elect, that they also may obtain salvation in Christ Jesus" (2 Tim. 2:10). This verse shows that even though He knew He would be persecuted for doing so, He was motivated by the realization that there were other future believers who would accept Christ as Savior upon hearing the gospel (cf. Rom. 10: 14, 15). In fact, once that last person has been born again, Jesus will return (cf. 2 Pet. 2:13).

Q: How come Christians do not seem to care about the environment?

A: It is unfortunate that in many circles there is a perception that Christians do not care about our environment. I, for one, agree with Francis Schaeffer who said, "Christians, of all people, should not be destroyers. We should treat nature with an overwhelming respect. Because I love God, I love what he has made and I have respect for what he has made."[6] Genesis 1:28-31 shows that we are unique from creation and that we are to be stewards of it. The Bible also tells us that God takes pleasure in his creation (Ps. 104:24-30; Mt. 6:26).

To answer your question, I believe that most Christians *do care* about the environment, but less emphasis is placed upon it because of the greater priority of the Great Commission (Mt. 28:19-20; Acts 1:8). Jesus came to seek and to save the lost (Lk. 19:10), but God's plan of redemption does include blessings for the whole earth (Rom. 8:19-23).

I believe that becoming more environmentally-mindful may indeed open a few doors for a gospel presentation to those who are ecologically-conscious, and that as a whole we can do a better job while remaining focused on the higher priority of making disciples.

---

[6]Francis Schaeffer, *Pollution and the Death of Man* (Wheaton: Crossway Books, 1970).

32

Tithing

Q: In church you said the Bible doesn't specify how much we should tithe as long as we do it with a pure heart. Did I misunderstand? I've always been told we should tithe ten percent of our income, and I understand that there are references in the Bible to support this. Can you clarify this for me? I've been tithing but I don't give ten percent. I was told that if I didn't tithe ten percent that I would never be blessed by God.

A: Because of Jesus Christ we are no longer bound to tithe ten percent of our finances, nor the firstborn of our livestock, etc. The entire Mosaic Law comes to fulfillment in Christ, and this fulfillment means that the Law is no longer a direct and immediate source of or judge of the conduct of God's people. Christian behavior is now guided directly by the "law of Christ."

In Acts, for example, the early Church emphasized tithing in different ways and in varying degrees that went beyond monetary donations, and included the giving of one's time and talents for God's work (see Acts 2:44-45). The percentage is not as important as the fact that you are indeed investing in the Kingdom of God through your finances, time, and talents. Paul spells out the New Testament principle of giving as stewardship of all that we have (2 Cor. 9:6-15).

Q: Your "Enlarge Out Hearts" drive has totally confused my understanding of biblical tithing. I was taught from the Bible that we had to give only ten percent of our net income and that anything extra was considered a special love offering. What is SBC's official position on how much of my income I am required to give back to God?

A: Giving in the New Testament entails more of a trustee concept because technically nothing we own is really ours but gifts from God. Interestingly, the New Testament words translated most often as "steward" (*epitropos* and *oikonomos*) are better understood as trustees.

In my opinion, the concept of giving back to God misleads us into thinking that our "gifts" are ours in the first place. The truth is the exact opposite. Everything we have is a trust from God. Technically trustees own nothing, but nevertheless are legally accountable for everything under their supervision: time, talents, capital, etc. (see Mt. 25:14-30). This was the concept that the early Church practiced in Acts 2. All of that to say that I try to practice Jesus' instruction of "Freely you have received, freely give" (Mt. 10:8).

In regard to ten percent, we are no longer under the Old Testament Law and thus no longer bound to a ten percent tithe any more than we are the dietary restrictions, etc. In reality, the typical Hebrew gave more than ten percent through temple taxes, various feasts, etc., but the more important issue with Jesus is that whatever percentage you give that it is not given begrudgingly. Regardless of the amount that you can "freely give" it should be given in the spirit of the poor widow (see Mk. 12:41-44).

33

The Trinity

Q: I simply cannot seem to comprehend the Trinity. To me it sounds like a polytheistic belief. How can God be three-in-one without being more than one? Any suggestions on how to finally resolve the way I "think" about God?

A: Thanks for being so honest. The Trinity is indeed a mystery and thus a difficult concept to grasp. In fact, Tertullian argued that the Trinity was proof of God's existence because such a concept would be impossible for humans to construct. Scripture provides revelation on the Trinity showing us that the one Godhead exists simultaneously in three persons. It is one of the truly distinctive doctrines of Christianity in that God is one and yet there are three who make up the Godhead (cf. Isa. 48:12-16; 2 Cor. 13:4; Heb. 1:1-9).

There have been various attempts to create anthropomorphisms to explain the Trinity. For example, imagine a rainbow of just three colors. It is one rainbow, and yet it is distinctly three different colors. These illustrations shed some light on the concept of the Trinity. However, like all illustrations, it is inherently deficient because it is an *illustration* rather than the *original*. It is a view of the original and simply cannot do complete justice in explaining the concept. What we do know is that the Trinity is clearly taught in Scripture. We see God saying in Genesis 1:26, "Let us make man in our image." Likewise, in Matthew 3:16-17 we simultaneously see all three members of the Godhead at the baptism of Jesus: Father, Son, and Holy Spirit.

Q: Why do we need to believe that Jesus and the Holy Spirit are God? What basis is there to believe that they are empowered agents of God? Jesus repeatedly differentiates Himself from the Father (He that sent Me). In John 14:28 Jesus said, "My Father is greater than I." How could all three be one God, yet one be greater than the other?

A: The doctrine of the Trinity is crucial to Christian theology. Although the Trinity finds its clearest evidence in the New Testament, the doctrine of the Trinity is seen throughout the Bible. The plural form of the name of God (*Elohim*), as well as the use of plural pronouns to refer to God (Gen. 1:26; 11:7), point in this direction. There are numerous passages that cite and confirm the Triune nature of God. God is one (Deut. 6:4; Gal. 3:20; Jam. 2:19), but the Son (Jn. 1:1; 14:9; Col. 2:9) and the Holy Spirit (Acts 5:3-4; 1 Cor. 3:16) are also fully God. They are, however, distinct from the Father and one another.

The Father sent the Son and the Spirit (Jn. 15:26; Gal. 4:4). This unified equality and distinctness is regularly seen in the references such as the one you listed. The situation that you referenced in John 14:28, for example, shows the difference in office. The Father is "greater" in office, but not in nature, since both are God (Jn. 1:1; 8:58; 10:30). (This is similar to male and female and the "office" of husband and wife). Thus Jesus is equal to the Father in essence, nature, and character, and yet different in function and office. The Trinitarian doctrine is also central to the doctrine of salvation, in which God acts personally in history to redeem and share Himself with humanity, and this is why we baptize "in the name of the Father, Son, and Holy Spirit" (Mt. 28:19).

34

UFOs

Q: Did Ezekiel see a UFO in Ezekiel 1?

A: Initially, these passages about flying wheels do indeed sound like an ancient UFO report, and UFO enthusiasts regularly cite them in an attempt to verify their claims of extraterrestrial interventions in the course of human history. However, a closer examination of the text clearly demonstrates that Ezekiel is communicating a *vision* from God and not an extraterrestrial visitation. We violate a number of basic principles of biblical interpretation (hermeneutics) if we assume that the wheels of Ezekiel are spaceships.

First, we must read the passage within its entire context, and second we must attempt to interpret what the biblical author is trying to communicate to his intended audience. With this in mind we see that this passage is the first of several visions. Events seen in visions are not necessarily literal, but are often symbolic or metaphorical. In this case the creatures and wheels are most likely representations of angels who are presented as God's attendants.

Most Bible scholars concur that the wheels are a vision intended to encourage Ezekiel by reminding him of God's attribute of omnipresence. Since the Kebar River (the location of the vision) was probably South of Babylon and a place of prayer for the Jewish exiles, this vision would have been most appropriate at this site to remind Israel that wherever they went, God went...even in Babylon.

Q: Would the proof of ET and UFOs undermine the basic theological foundations of Christianity?

A: No. If they *do* exist, God is their Creator too. According to Genesis

1:1, "God created the heavens and the earth." Therefore, such a discovery would *not* nullify Christian doctrine, but rather confirm the extent of God's creative capabilities. It is very clear from Scripture and from creation that God delights in being creative. For example, when He created angels He did not create just one type, but rather a variety. Nevertheless, we do know that humanity is unique in that we have been created in the image of God (Gen. 1:26).

Although I personally do not believe in the existence of other civilizations outside of planet earth, nor is there any tangible evidence to suggest their existence, it should not come as a huge surprise to Christians if there are other life forms in the universe. However, the bottom line for humanity is the fact that, regardless of the existence of ET, we on earth are spiritually corrupt and in need of a Savior for forgiveness and everlasting life which is only available through Jesus Christ.

35

Video Games

Q: What is your view on video games that have demons in them?

A: My primary concern would be a child developing an unhealthy fascination with the occult, violence, and the paranormal. Therefore, I would opt to substitute it with a non-occultic game. Read 1 Corinthians 8:1-13. You can replace "food" with the video games.

Women

Q: I am a woman with the gift of teaching. I understand that SBC holds the position that women are not allowed to teach men. (I understand the idea of headship of the husband and that in the presence of her husband there is a different context.) This is a position with which I personally agree. However, I have at times needed to defend this position to others, even within our church. What exactly is SBC's official position? When is it okay for women to teach men? When is it not? I know the Scriptures in 1 Corinthians 14 and 1 Timothy 2, but the usual response to them is that they were just cultural. Can you help me with a better way to communicate the reason for my conviction? Thanks.

A: Thanks for the question and your spirit. It is our position at SBC that women are equal to men and that they can and should serve in any ministry position in the church with the exception of a position that would give them ecclesiastical authority over a man (1 Cor. 11:13; 1 Tim. 2:11-14). Thus a woman is not to serve as an elder or pastor over men. All other positions are carried out by men and women based on their giftedness.

37

Worship

Q: Often after hearing a soloist or the orchestra present a piece beautifully many people in the congregation clap. And often I feel like joining them. Obviously, the response is applauding the performance. I believe our purpose in worship should be to bring glory to the Name of God alone. Since SBC evidently allows the applause for the performer, how do you reconcile this with the purpose of worship?

A: All I can say is that for me personally, I clap unto the Lord out of gratefulness for what was given in worship and not at the performance itself. Occasionally, I have applauded a testimony or musical performance as a tangible way of saying *amen* in that I am grateful for their service and ministry in praising God with their gifts, talents, or testimony, but it is all because of what God has done and is doing in their lives. Thus, it is an exaltation of God and not the performer.

Bibliography

Brewer, Bobby. *Postmodernism: What You Should Know and Do About It* (New York: Writer's Showcase, 2001).

Brown, Walt. *In the Beginning: Compelling Evidence for Creation and the Flood* (Phoenix, Arizona: Center for Scientific Creation, 7th Edition, 2001).

Duthie, Alan S. *How to Choose Your Bible Wisely* (Carlisle, United Kingdom: Paternoster Press, 2nd Edition, 1995).

Grudem, Wayne. *Systematic Theology* (Grand Rapids: Zondervan, 1994).

Hanegraaff, Hank. *The FACE that Demonstrates the Farce of Evolution* (NashVille: Word, 1998).

Hybels, Bill. *Becoming A Contagious Christian* (Grand Rapids: Zondervan, 1995).

McDowell, Josh. *More than a Carpenter* (Wheaton: Tyndale, 1977).

Olson, Roger E. *The Story of Christian Theology* (Downers Grove, IL: InterVarsity Press, 1999).

Schaeffer, Francis. *Pollution and the Death of Man* (Wheaton, Crossway Books, 1970).

Strobel, Lee. *The Case for Christ* (Grand Rapids: Zondervan, 1998).

_____. *The Case for Faith* (Grand Rapids: Zondervan, 2000).

Wegner, Paul. *The Journey from Texts to Translations: The Origin and Development of the Bible* (Grand Rapids: Baker Books, 2000).

Glossary

Apologetics. A term used to describe the rational defense of Christian doctrine.

Creationism. The belief that creation occurred as a direct and willful act of God as described in Genesis 1-2.

Darwinism. The belief in evolution as described by Charles Darwin (1809-1882).

Dispensationalism. The belief that there are seven different historical periods (dispensations) in how God related and revealed Himself to His creation. It was first articulated by J.N. Darby in the nineteenth century and also emphasizes a distinction between the Church and Israel as the two primary groups for God's redemptive plans for humanity.

Eschatology. The biblical study of the end times.

Exclusivism. The belief that salvation is only available for those who have faith in Christ. Sometimes referred to as Particularism.

Evangelical. A term used today to refer to Christians who hold to a theology that is connected with the gospel of Jesus Christ and Essential Christian Doctrine.

Foreknowledge. God's knowledge of future events, including human choices.

Free Will. The ability of humanity to make choices within the sovereignty of God.

Hermeneutics. The discipline of biblical interpretation.

Immutability. A divine attribute of God indicating his perfection in that He is unchangeable.

Incarnation. A term to reference when God the Son became human in the person of Jesus Christ.

Inerrancy. The belief that the original biblical manuscripts were without error.

Omnipotence. The attribute and quality of God of being all-powerful.

Omnipresence. The attribute and quality of God of simultaneously being present everywhere.

Omniscience. The attribute and quality of God of being all-knowing.

Pluralism. The belief that any and/or all moral religions lead to God.

Postmodernism. A term used to describe both a worldview and era (1972-Present) of loosely connected trends, ideologies, and cultural characteristics which primarily embrace relativism, pluralism, spiritual curiosity, and a general ignorance and suspicion of Christian beliefs.

Predestination. The belief that God has sovereignly predetermined for all of history who will be elected or saved.

Relativism. The belief that morality and religion are determined by one's social setting and background, and thus relativism denies any absolute or objective standards.

Revelation. What God has revealed about Himself to humanity.

Theodicy. The attempt to answer how and/or why a holy God would allow the existence of evil.

Theology. The study of God.

Worldview. A set of presuppositions which may be true, false, or a blend of both that a person holds about the general makeup of the world, life, God, etc.

About the Authors

Darryl DelHousaye (pronounced DEL-who-say) (D.Min., Western Seminary; M.Div., Talbot School of Theology; Senior Pastor of Scottsdale Bible Church, Scottsdale, Arizona) has a gift for presenting the Word of God with infectious joy and a genuine love for God's truth. Because of his broad experience with the Christian community, Darryl is able to combine maturity with an understanding of the conflicts that confront various age groups, enabling him to communicate effectively with all generations. Married thirty-two years to his wife, Holly, Darryl has enjoyed God's richest gift in a fulfilling and rewarding relationship with his family. Darryl is also author of the book, *Today for Eternity*, published by J. Christopher Publishing, Inc., and authored the study notes for the Book of Acts in the *Nelson Study Bible*, published by Thomas Nelson Publishers.

Bobby Brewer (D.Min., Phoenix Seminary; M.Div., Liberty Baptist Theological Seminary, Lynchburg, Virginia) is Minister of Community Outreach and Church Growth at Scottsdale Bible Church. He is the author of *Postmodernism: What You Should Know and Do About It*. He and his wife, Kristen, have been members of SBC since 1992.